Louisiana Place Names of Indian Origin

Fire Ant Books

Louisiana Place Names of Indian Origin

A Collection of Words

William A. Read

Edited and with an Introduction by
George M. Riser

THE UNIVERSITY OF ALABAMA PRESS

Tuscaloosa

Typeface: ACaslon

∞

The paper on which this book is printed meets the minimum requirements of
American National Standard for Information Sciences-Permanence of Paper for
Printed Library Materials, ANSI Z39.48-1984.

Library of Congress Cataloging-in-Publication Data

Read, William A.
    Louisiana place names of Indian origin : a collection of words / William A. Read ;
edited and with an Introduction by George M. Riser.
        p.   cm.
        "Fire Ant books."
    Collection of 3 previously published articles by the author.
    Includes bibliographical references.
    ISBN 978-0-8173-5505-0 (pbk. : alk. paper) — ISBN 978-0-8173-8072-4
(electronic) 1. Names, Indian—Louisiana. 2. Names, Geographical—Louisiana.
I. Title.
    E78.L8R43 2008
    917.63—dc22

                                                                    2008005570

Contents

Illustrations

1. William A. Read

Introduction

Louisiana Place Names of Indian Origin, originally published in 1927, was the first in a series of studies William A. Read undertook to examine place names of Indian origin in different southern states. The current reissue of the Louisiana volume is designed to complement studies by William A. Read previously reprinted by The University of Alabama Press: *Florida Place Names of Indian Origin and Seminole Personal Names,* originally published in 1934, and *Indian Place Names in Alabama,* originally published in 1937. Although largely unknown today, William A. Read was an accomplished scholar whose legacy extends well beyond the information preserved in this series of books. The purpose of this introduction is to provide background about his professional life and the academic milieu in which he spent his career.

William Alexander Read was born in Virginia four years after Lee surrendered at Appomattox and died ninety-three years later, while John F. Kennedy was president of the United States. For thirty-eight years, from 1902 to 1940, Dr. Read chaired the English Department at Louisiana State University, where he was revered by his students. His official title, Professor of the English Language and Literature, conveys a sense of his approach to teaching, for Dr. Read instilled in his students an appreciation of the power of words to create meaningful literature. Today, the William A. Read Professor of English is an endowed chair at LSU that confers a status of excellence and distinction.

Dr. Read first and foremost was a philologist in its literal sense, a lover of words, whether spoken or written. Having received his Ph.D. from the University of Heidelberg in 1897, Dr. Read soon published scholarly articles in German journals as well as in the *Journal of English and German*

Philology. After arriving in Louisiana in 1902, he began to study words used both by Native Americans and by the Francophone residents of Louisiana. Apparently believing these unique vocabularies were in the process of disappearing, Dr. Read made a concerted effort to record and document the meaning of words used by both indigenous populations. Following the publication of his study of Indian place names, his next publication, in 1931, was *Louisiana-French*, the term Dr. Read used for the French dialect peculiar to Louisiana. Primarily a monograph defining many unusual French words heard in Louisiana, often applied to the natural environment, this publication remains a valuable reference for anyone interested in the history of the three southern states, Alabama, Mississippi, and Louisiana, where documents pertaining to early European settlement were written in French.

Even after retiring from LSU at the age of seventy-one, Dr. Read continued to pursue his research interests. At eighty, he published "Indian Stream-Names in Georgia" in the *International Journal of American Linguistics* and one year later followed with "Indian Stream-Names in Georgia II" in the same journal. The recently published *Native American Place Names in Mississippi* (Baca 2007), moreover, incorporates place name data collected for a doctoral thesis directed by Dr. Read in 1939 but never before published. Other than researchers affiliated with the Bureau of American Ethnology, Dr. Read probably did more to preserve a record of Native American vocabularies in the Southeast than anyone else in the twentieth century.

In addition to teaching students and conducting research, Dr. Read had administrative responsibilities in the English Department that required both time and a certain amount of diplomacy. In his role as head of the department, Dr. Read fundamentally was a nineteenth-century European scholar called on to maintain a stable academic environment in the turbulence of twentieth-century America. The fact that he succeeded was perhaps one of his most impressive accomplishments.

Economically, the years before World War II were particularly trying in the United States. Beginning during the late 1920s, the LSU campus in Baton Rouge became a center of political ferment that eventually spilled out over the borders of Louisiana. To understand the importance of Dr. Read's reassuring presence during these turbulent years, some background is needed about the exceptional cast of characters who also appeared on the LSU campus during this period.

In 1928, with the Louisiana economy still shattered by the Great Mississippi River Flood of 1927, Huey P. Long was elected governor of Louisiana by espousing a brand of radical populism that soon began to resonate with Americans mired in the ongoing despair of the Great Depression. Partly in response to a highly vocal Huey Long, then a U.S. senator, the Roosevelt administration promoted programs such as the Works Progress Administration in which the federal government assumed responsibility for employing people unable to find work in the private sector. An increasingly powerful Senator Long meanwhile became a virtual dictator in Louisiana, extending his activities to include even directing the LSU band and advising the LSU football coach about which plays to call.

In 1935, shortly before Huey Long was assassinated, two young faculty members Dr. Read had added to the English Department, Cleanth Brooks and Robert Penn Warren, helped found the *Southern Review* as a spin-off of the *Southwest Review,* then jointly published with Southern Methodist University in Texas. Between 1935 and 1942, before publication was suspended because of World War II, this innovative quarterly attracted contributions from, among others, Mark Van Doren, T. S. Eliot, W. H. Auden, Wallace Stevens, John Crowe Ransom, Aldous Huxley, Allen Tate, and Ford Madox Ford. The *Southern Review* also gave a voice to many aspiring women writers of the time: Mary McCarthy, Katherine Ann Porter, Caroline Gordon, and a young lady living quietly in Mississippi named Eudora Welty. In compensation for their work on the *Southern Review,* each of its two managing editors, Cleanth Brooks and Robert Penn Warren, was allowed to reduce his teaching load in the English Department by one-quarter.

The flagship university of Louisiana achieved some degree of national and international renown through the wide circulation of the *Southern Review.* As Brooks and Warren later noted (1953), subscriptions came from "the Middle South, New York and the East, and the West Coast. There was, relatively speaking, a large circulation in England. Calcutta and Tokyo, as the editors were once forced to notice, had, either of them, more subscribers than Atlanta, Georgia. The editors never quite decided what this meant about their self-appointed mission." The editors also never quite decided what was meant by a "southern" writer: "Once, after the magazine had been operating for several years, the editors, out of mere curiosity, did make a check on the local origins of their contributors. About 51 percent were southern. But the word southern is, in itself, not too clear. Is Oklahoma, or Kentucky, southern? It is hard to say."

Dr. Read's interest in the vocabularies of southern Indians was complemented by developments that occurred on another part of the LSU campus. When the School of Geology hired Fred B. Kniffen as an assistant professor in 1927, the LSU faculty gained its first member with an interest in anthropology. Largely because of Dr. Kniffen's presence in the School of Geology, a highly focused young man from Mississippi, James A. Ford, found an academic home on the LSU campus. Enrolling as a student in 1934, Mr. Ford earned his B.A from LSU in 1936.

When articles Kniffen and Ford had written for the *Louisiana Conservation Review* were particularly well received—an article about the historic Indian tribes of Louisiana by Kniffen and two about the archaeology of Louisiana by Ford—the Louisiana Department of Conservation decided to publish a series of studies devoted exclusively to anthropology. In what may be an example of unintended consequences, the first three anthropological studies published by the Louisiana Department of Conservation (Ford 1935, 1936; Ford and Willey 1940) profoundly and forever altered the course of American archaeology.

Having established a systematic approach to classifying fragments of pottery as a way to clarify the change through time of prehistoric human culture—after having established a scientific foundation for the development of a distinct Americanist archaeology—Ford was given an appointment as a research associate in the LSU School of Geology. Beginning in the fall of 1937, he took a nine-month leave to earn an M.A. at the University of Michigan before returning to his position at LSU. Between 1938 and 1940, Ford organized and directed a joint LSU-WPA archaeological project that employed hundreds of unskilled workers and a cadre of talented young archaeologists, one of whom was Gordon R. Willey.

Prior to coauthoring *The Crooks Site* (Ford and Willey 1940), Gordon Willey had published articles primarily about the somewhat dubious use of dendrochronology as a means of measuring time in the prehistoric Southeast. After leaving Louisiana in 1940, Willey traveled east and applied what he had learned from Ford about measuring change through time to the prehistoric pottery of Florida. Other publications eventually followed.

In 1940, William A. Read retired from LSU; in 1942, publication of the *Southern Review* was suspended because of the war; in 1946, Robert Penn Warren, who had moved on when the *Southern Review* became dormant, published *All the King's Men* and picked up a Pulitzer Prize; in 1947, Cleanth Brooks also moved on and subsequently had a distinguished career as a literary critic. In 1946, James A. Ford resigned as a research associate at LSU and moved to New York to become Curator of North American

Archaeology at the American Museum of Natural History. In 1949, while in New York, Mr. Ford finally took time to earn a Ph.D. from Columbia University. Before long, Ford and Willey were two of the most highly esteemed archaeologists in North America.

When Dr. Read ended his tenure at LSU in 1940, his retirement was recognized by the publication of *Studies for William A. Read: A Miscellany Presented by Some of His Colleagues and Friends* (Caffee and Kirby 1940). Written by a variety of people Dr. Read had influenced and befriended during the early decades of the twentieth century, this book is divided into two sections, Language and Literature, and contains contributions from twenty-four authors. Most of the articles are of a highly specialized nature; two are written in German. The final article in the literature section is titled "The First Description of an Indian Tribe in the Territory of the Present United States" and was written by Dr. Read's good friend at the Smithsonian, John R. Swanton. In this article, Dr. Swanton reassesses the Chicora legend and, contrary to his earlier conclusions, argues for accepting much of this "legend" as being true—a conclusion shared by a scholar later affiliated with LSU, Paul E. Hoffman, as detailed in *A New Andalucia and a Way to the Orient* (1990).

As early as 1927, when *Louisiana Place Names of Indian Origin* was published, Dr. Read and Dr. Swanton were exchanging information about Native American linguistics, for several references to Dr. Swanton can be found in the book that follows. Their careers probably intersected at some point after 1911 when Dr. Swanton published the map that appears on the cover of this book, a foldout insert from *Indian Tribes of the Lower Mississippi Valley and Adjacent Coast of the Gulf of Mexico*. For two serious scholars who had a concurrent interest in the same subject—Native American linguistics in Louisiana, Mississippi, and Alabama—each must have found in the other a colleague with whom to share bits of linguistic data that others might have found slightly less than fascinating. The fact that Dr. Swanton made an effort to contribute to a book commemorating Dr. Read's retirement suggests a close working relationship of long duration.

Like Dr. Swanton, Dr. Read was interested in the phonetic structure of Indian words; each word in the book that follows includes information about its pronunciation, about how it was meant to sound. With the change through time of the languages heard in Louisiana—from that of the Indians to that of the Francophones to that of the Anglophones—there seems to have been a steady decline in the intrinsic appeal, if not in the intrinsic beauty, of words. *Louisiana Place Names of Indian Origin* serves as a

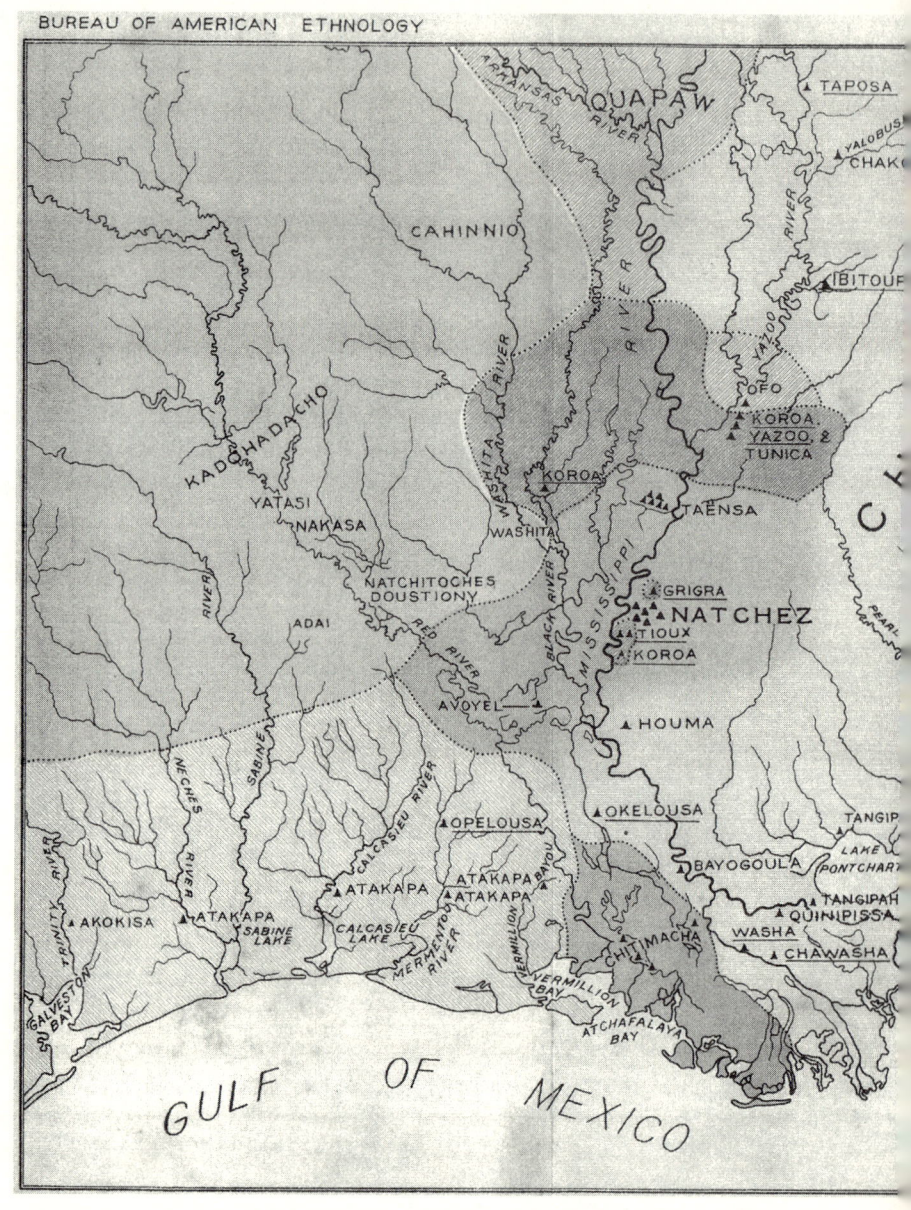

2. Indian tribes of the Lower Mississippi and adjacent Gulf Coast

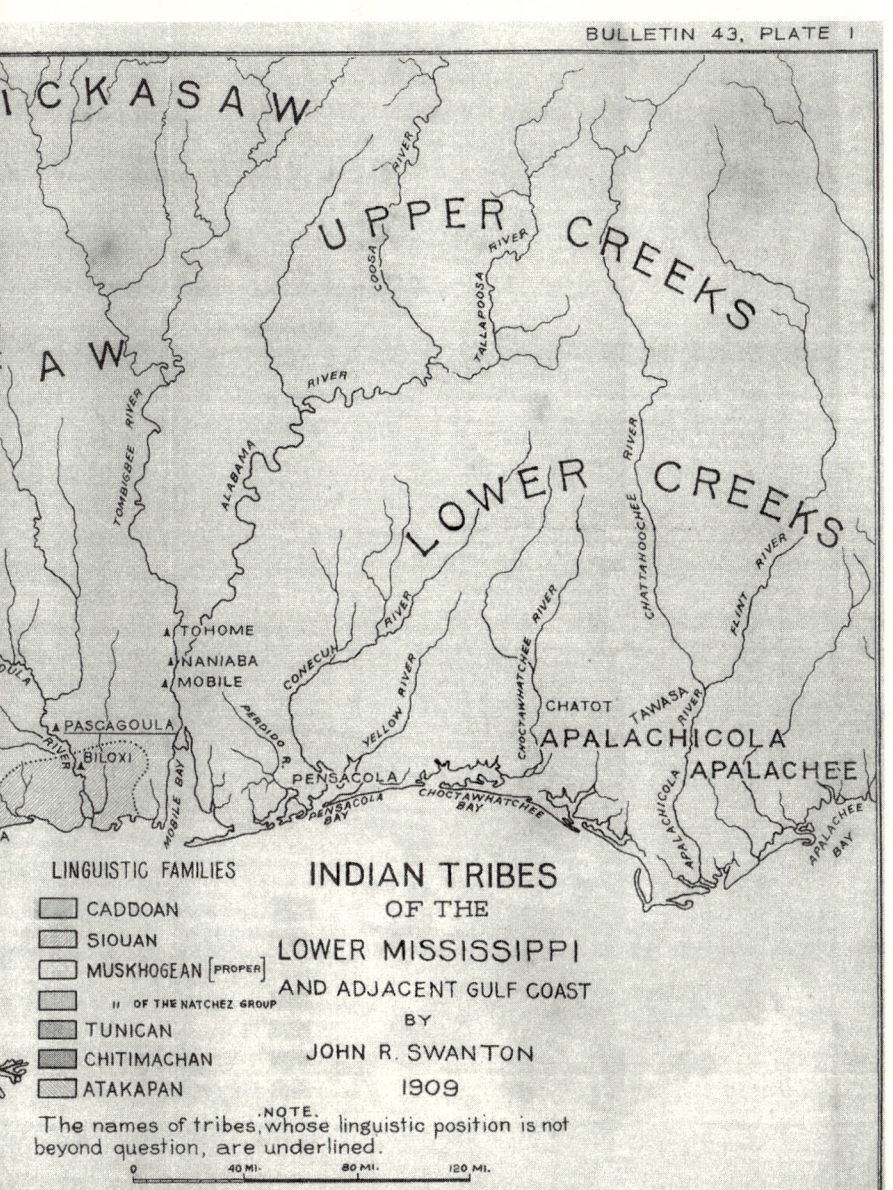

ICKASAW

UPPER CREEKS

LOWER CREEKS

AW

RIVER

COOSA RIVER

TALLAPOOSA RIVER

RIVER

CHATTAHOOCHEE RIVER

FLINT RIVER

TOMBIGBEE RIVER

ALABAMA

RIVER

CONECUH

PERDIDO R.

YELLOW RIVER

CHOCTAWHATCHEE RIVER

CHATOT

TAWASA RIVER

APALACHICOLA

APALACHICOLA RIVER

APALACHEE

▲TOHOME
▲NANIABA
▲MOBILE

▲PASCAGOULA
RIVER
▲BILOXI

OULA

A

MOBILE BAY

PENSACOLA

PENSACOLA BAY

CHOCTAWHATCHEE BAY

APALACHEE BAY

LINGUISTIC FAMILIES

☐ CADDOAN
☐ SIOUAN
☐ MUSKHOGEAN [PROPER]
☐ II OF THE NATCHEZ GROUP
☐ TUNICAN
☐ CHITIMACHAN
☐ ATAKAPAN

INDIAN TRIBES
OF THE
LOWER MISSISSIPPI
AND ADJACENT GULF COAST
BY
JOHN R. SWANTON
1909

NOTE.
The names of tribes, whose linguistic position is not
beyond question, are underlined.

0   40 MI.   80 MI.   120 MI.

reminder of yet another way Native Americans enrich our surroundings—and not just in Louisiana. Place names of Indian origin, often overlooked, represent one of the most obvious imprints left on the American landscape by Native Americans.

Dr. Read essentially was a lover of words who made collections to be displayed and shared with the public. The book that follows is divided into three sections corresponding to three collections of words Dr. Read published over a short period of time: *Louisiana Place Names of Indian Origin,* 1927; "More Indian Place Names in Louisiana," 1928; and a chapter in *Louisiana-French* titled "Indian words," 1931. The page numbers from the original publications appear in brackets. Read's text is reproduced verbatim except for silent correction of a few obvious typographical errors. Although he began his career as a philologist, publishing articles in a journal of philology, Dr. Read eventually and perhaps unintentionally became a linguist, publishing articles in a journal of linguistics at the end of his career. Even in the study of words, things apparently change. Were the content of this book to be submitted for publication in a modern journal, it probably would find a home in a journal of semiotics.

Perhaps even more important than his collections of words were the long-remembered lessons Dr. Read taught on the LSU campus. In his classes, Dr. Read emphasized that words not only were interesting but also had practical value—that words were just as powerful as bullets and generally were to be preferred in a civil society. As professor of the English Language and Literature, Dr. Read taught that words were relied on to create meaningful literature and subsequently had his students read and discover examples.

The book that follows can be read on many levels: as a study in semiotics, as a study in linguistics, as a study in geography, or as a collection of interesting words. It can be read as a book written by a southern writer, as a book about the Southeast, as a book about Native Americans, or as a book about the history of Louisiana. Alternatively, forgetting all expectations, the reader can simply enjoy this book because it is engaging and contains interesting nuggets of knowledge waiting to be discovered between its covers. In that sense, the reader may even find something resembling a meaningful work of literature in the pages that follow.

George M. Riser
August 2008

REFERENCES CITED

Baca, Keith A. 2007. *Native American Place Names in Mississippi.* University Press of Mississippi, Jackson.

Brooks, Cleanth, and Robert Penn Warren. 1953. *An Anthology of Stories from the Southern Review.* Louisiana State University Press, Baton Rouge.

Caffee, Nathaniel M., and Thomas A. Kirby. 1940. *Studies for William A. Read: A Miscellany Presented by Some of His Colleagues and Friends.* Louisiana State University Press, Baton Rouge.

Ford, James A. 1935. Anthropological Study no. 1: *A Ceramic Decoration Sequence at an Old Indian Village Site near Sicily Island, Louisiana.* Louisiana Department of Conservation, Baton Rouge.

———. 1936. Anthropological Study no. 2: *Analysis of Indian Village Site Collections from Louisiana and Mississippi.* Louisiana Department of Conservation, Baton Rouge.

Ford, James A., and Gordon R. Willey. 1940. Anthropological Study no. 3: *Crooks Site: A Marksville Period Burial Mound in LaSalle Parish, Louisiana.* Louisiana Department of Conservation, Baton Rouge.

Hoffman, Paul A. 1990. *A New Andalucia and a Way to the Orient.* Louisiana State University Press, Baton Rouge.

Read, William A. 1927. *Louisiana Place Names of Indian Origin.* University Bulletin, Louisiana State University and Agricultural and Mechanical College, vol. XIX, n.s., no. 2. The Collegiate Press, George Banta Publishing Co., Menasha, Wisconsin.

———. 1931. *Louisiana-French.* Louisiana State University Studies no. 5. Louisiana State University Press, Baton Rouge.

———. 1934. *Florida Place Names of Indian Origin and Seminole Personal Names.* Louisiana State University Studies no. 11. Louisiana State University Press, Baton Rouge.

———. 1937. *Indian Place Names in Alabama.* Louisiana State University Studies no. 29. Louisiana State University Press, Baton Rouge. Revised edition, 1984, The University of Alabama Press, Tuscaloosa.

———. 1949. "Indian Stream-Names in Georgia." *International Journal of American Linguistics* 15: 128–32.

———. 1950. "Indian Stream-Names in Georgia II." *International Journal of American Linguistics* 16: 203–7.

ABOUT THE EDITOR

George M. Riser has lived in Covington, Louisiana, for the past thirty years and is a retired internist. He has served on the Louisiana Antiquities Commission for over a decade and currently is president of the Louisiana Archaeological Society. Born in Monroe in 1941, he grew up hunting and fishing on the floodplain of northeastern Louisiana at a time when the only people who drove pick-up trucks were hardworking cotton farmers. His father was a football coach at Ouachita Parish High School when he met the author's mother, an English teacher at the same school. His mother graduated from LSU in 1928 with a major in English. One of the many books she treasured was the copy of *Louisiana Place Names of Indian Origin* used in the reissue of this edition.

WILLIAM ALEXANDER READ

Biographical Outline

1869: Born at Bristol, Virginia, November 17
1888: A.B., King College (Tennessee)
1892–94: University of Virginia
1894–95: University of Göttingen
1895–97: University of Heidelberg
1897: Ph.D., Heidelberg
1898–99: Johns Hopkins University
1899–1900: University of Arkansas, associate professor of English and modern languages
1900–1902: University of Arkansas, professor of English and modern languages
1902–1940: Louisiana State University, professor of English and head of the department
1908: University of Grenoble
1909: Oxford University

Professional Activities

American Dialect Society
English Place-Name Society
Linguistic Society of America
Committee of the Modern Language Association to Survey Place-Name Study in America
Committee on the Linguistic Atlas of the United States and Canada
American Correspondent for the *Zeitschrift für Ortsnamenforschung*
Editor of the *Southwest Review*, 1932–35
Vice-President, Louisiana Historical Society
Member of the Editorial and Pronunciation Committees of the *Thorndike–Century Senior Dictionary*
Modern Language Association of America

Bibliography

Books and Pamphlets

Keats and Spenser, Heidelberg, 1897.
The Southern R (Louisiana State University Bulletin, I, n.s., no. 2), Baton Rouge, 1910. (Reprinted from *Louisiana School Review,* February 1910.)

Some Variant Pronunciations in the New South (Louisiana State University Bulletin, III, n.s., no. 5), Baton Rouge, 1912. (Reprinted from *Dialect Notes,* III, no. 7, 1911.)

A Vernerian Sound Change in English, paper read at the meeting of the New Orleans Academy of Sciences, April 15, 1913; Leipzig, 1914. (Reprinted from *Englische Studien,* XLVII, 1913.)

Louisiana Place Names of Indian Origin (Louisiana State University Bulletin, XIX, n.s., no. 2), Baton Rouge, 1927.

Indian Place Names in Louisiana, n.p., 1928.

Louisiana-French (Louisiana State University Studies, no. 5), Baton Rouge: Louisiana State University Press, 1931.

Florida Place Names of Indian Origin and Seminole Personal Names (Louisiana State University Studies, no. 11), Baton Rouge: Louisiana State University Press, 1934. Revised edition, 2004, The University of Alabama Press, Tuscaloosa.

Indian Place Names in Alabama (Louisiana State University Studies, no. 29), Baton Rouge: Louisiana State University Press, 1937. Revised edition, 1984, The University of Alabama Press, Tuscaloosa.

Articles

"Modern English *ajar,*" *Modern Language Notes* XVI (April 1901), 127.

"Keats and Spenser," *Modern Language Notes* XVIII (November 1903), 204–6.

"A Note on Nasalized Vowels," *Modern Language Notes* XX (May 1905), 159–60.

"Notes on the University of Oxford," *The Alumnus* V (October 1909), 23–27.

"The Vowel System of the Southern United States," *Englische Studien* XLI (1910), 70–78.

"The Southern R," *Louisiana School Review* (February 1910).

"Some Variant Pronunciations in the New South," *Dialect Notes* III (1911), 497–536.

"A Vernerian Sound Change in English," *Englische Studien* XLVII (1913), 167–84.

"Chaucer's *Troilus and Criseyde,* I, 228," *Journal of English and Germanic Philology* XX (July 1921), 397–98.

"Some Phases of American Pronunciation," *Journal of English and Germanic Philology* XXII (April 1923), 217–44.

"Some Remarks on American Pronunciations," *The Journal of the Louisiana Teachers' Association* II (May 1925), 41–45.

"Creole and Cajan," *American Speech* I, n.s. (June 1926), 483.

"Research in American Place Names, c. 1920–1926: A Partial Review," *Zeitschrift für Ortsnamenforschung* IV (1928), 185–91.

"More Indian Place Names in Louisiana," *Louisiana Historical Quarterly* XI (July 1928), 445–62.

"A Correction," *Englische Studien* LXV (1930), 176.

"Istrouma," *Louisiana Historical Quarterly* XIV (October 1931), 503–15.

"Research in American Place Names since 1928," *Zeitschrift für Ortsnamenforschung* X (1934), 222–42.

"Henry Plauché Dart: In Memoriam" (Address of Dr. William A. Read), *Louisiana Historical Quarterly* XVIII (April 1935), 250–51.

"Some Louisiana-French Words," *Zeitschrift für französische Sprache und Literatur* LXI (May 1937), 63–84.

"Ten Alabama Place Names," *American Speech* XIII (February 1938), 79–80.

"The Hitchiti Name of Silver Springs, Florida," *Modern Language Notes* LIII (November 1938), 513.

"A Score of Louisiana-French Words," *Zeitschrift für französische Sprache and Literatur* LXIII (1939), 42–64.

"Notes on *A Dictionary of American English*, Parts I–VI," *American Speech* XIV (December 1939), 255–60.

"Notes on an Opelousas Manuscript of 1862," *American Anthropologist* (July 1940).

"Indian Stream-Names in Georgia," *International Journal of American Linguistics* (1949) 15:128–32.

"Indian Stream-Names in Georgia II," *International Journal of American Linguistics* (1950) 16:203–7.

Reviews

Kluge and Lutz's *English Etymology, Englische Studien* XXVII (1900), 275–77.

Keat's *Hyperion* (ed. Hoops), *Modern Language Notes* XV (April 1900), 121–23.

Havelok (ed. Holthausen), *Journal of English and Germanic Philology* III (1901), 510–11.

Thomson's *Castle of Indolence* (ed. Cohen), *Englische Studien* XXIX (1901), 133–34.

Babbitt's *College Words and Phrases. Englische Studien* XXIX (1901), 275–77.

Liddell's *Chaucer: Prologue, Knightes Tale, Nonne Preestes Tale. Modern Language Notes* XVII (June 1902), 191–93.

Rippmann's *Sounds of Spoken English. Englische Studien* XXXVIII (1907), 286–88.

Emerson's *Middle English Reader. Literatur-Blatt für germanische und romanische Philologie* XXVIII, no. 5 (May 1907), 152–53.

Lloyd's *Northern English. Modern Language Notes* XXV (November 1910), 230–31.

Studies

Krapp's *Modern English: Its Growth and Present Use. Englische Studien* XLIII (1911), 426–32.

Kenyon's *American Pronunciation. Journal of English and Germanic Philology* XXIV (1925), 270–73.

S.P.E. Tract No. 30: Kurath, "American Pronunciation"; Barnes, "Words from the French-é, ée"; Bridges, "Pronunciation of Clothes, &c." *Englische Studien* LXIII (1929), 408–14.

Krapp's *A Comprehensive Guide to Good English. Englische Studien* LXIV (1929), 75–77.

Krapp's *The English Language in America. Englische Studien* LXIV (1929), 77–80.

Ditchy's *Les Acadiens louisianais et leur Parler. Zeitschrift für französische Sprache und Literatur* LVII (1933), 365–76.

Gould's *Oklahoma Place Names. The Southwest Review* XIX (April 1934), 346–48.

Tinker's *Louisiana's Earliest Poet. The Southwest Review* XIX (July 1934), Books section, 1–2.

Vestal's *New Sources of Indian History. The Southwest Review* XX (October 1934), Books section, 7–8.

Tinker's *Gombo*. New York *Herald-Tribune*, "Books," XIII, no. 13 (November 29, 1936), 29.

Kennedy's *Current English*. *Englishe Studien* LXXII (1938), 273–80.

Whitfield's *Louisiana French Folk Songs*. *American Speech* XV (February 1940), 87–88.

"French Echoes from Antilles and Tropical America," *Libro Julilar de Homenaje al Dr. Juan M. Dihigo* of the University of Havana. n.d.

Louisiana Place Names of Indian Origin

1
Louisiana Place Names of Indian Origin

PREFACE

[v] During the preparation of this study I have received help from many persons. I wish to express my cordial thanks to Mrs. T. P. Thompson for the privilege of using her fine library of Americana; to my colleagues, Professors James F. Broussard and Hoguet A. Major, for information with regard to certain Creole-French terms; to my colleague, Professor Walter Prichard, for assistance on the early history of Louisiana; to Mr. Cecil Bird for numerous suggestions, both timely and valuable; to Mr. Robert Glenk, Curator of the Louisiana State Museum, for the opportunity of studying some rare maps and volumes; to Professor Charles H. Grandgent for notes on the etymology of *grôler;* to Dr. John R. Swanton for the analysis of several Indian names; and especially, to Mr. William Beer,* Director of the Howard Memorial Library, for his scholarly and generous aid on the bibliography of my subject.

Many thanks are also due to those who have answered my inquiries concerning local history, geography, pronunciation, and legends. Those to whom I am chiefly indebted—I have not space to name them all—are the following:

Mr. Frank J. Burke, Land and Industrial Commissioner, Texas & Pacific railway; Mrs. C. L. Breazeale; Mr. Upshur P. Breazeale;** Mr. J. A.

---

*Died February 1, 1927.
**Died February 3, 1927.

Broussard; Mr. Carl Campbell, Chief Clerk, State Land Office; Mr. P. A. Cloutier; Mr. George P. Covington; Judge Clay Elliott; the Hon. Harvey E. Ellis; Miss Lucy Foote, Assistant Librarian, Louisiana State University; Mr. George T. Goodman; Mr. J. H. Gilfoil; Mr. Fred Grace, Registrar, State Land Office; Miss Lucille Grace, Assistant Recorder, State Land Office; Miss Marie Gross; Mr. S. L. Herold; Mr. A. P. Hopkins; Mr. Henry Jastremski, Secretary of the Louisiana Public Service Commission; Mr. D. F. Perkins, Chief Clerk, Dept. of Agriculture and Immigration; Professor E. D. Perkins; Miss Stella Pierce; Miss Lois Quinn; Professor E. S. Richardson; Senator William J. Sandoz; Mr. L. F. Sherer, Chief Clerk, Louisiana Public Service Commission; Mr. Robert Towles; Mr. Harry D. Wilson, Commissioner of Agriculture and Immigration, State of Louisiana.

William A. Read
Louisiana State University

[vii] CONTENTS

Louisiana has numerous place names of Indian origin. With relatively few exceptions these are derived from the Longtown dialect of the Choctaw language, a dialect which was spoken in the western part of the old Choctaw nation. The phonetic system of this dialect is not complicated: it is poor in the number of consonants, but rich in the number and character of its vowels. The consonants are [p], [b], [t], [k], [g], [f], [j], [l], [ḷ], [m], [n], [ŋ], [s], [ʃ], [tʃ], [w], and [h]. [g] seems to occur, however, solely in the word *bok* or *bog*, "creek," "bayou," "river," while [ŋ] arises only as a glide between a nasalized vowel and a following [k], as in [polāŋka], "finally." The voiceless [elcee], like that in Welsh, is accompanied by a distinct friction of the breath along the side or sides of the tongue. Another point worthy of mention is that in some words *m* is a substitute for *b*, as in *maleli* or *baleli*, "to run."

The Choctaw vowels are, [a:], [o:], [v:], [i:], [ʔ], [e:], [ɛ], and [ʌ]. [ʌ] is said to have the value either of *u* in *cub* or *a* in *sofa*. There are also five nasal vowels, [ā], [ō], [u], [ī], and [Î], as well as two diphthongs, [ai], and [aɪ], the latter resembling approximately the corresponding English sounds in *find* and *found*. Perhaps the most striking feature of this vowel system appears in the ease with which [o] alternates with [u], as in *oski, uski,* "cane," *homma, humma,* "red," *itola, itula,* "to fall," and many other words.

In words of two or three syllables the stress usually falls on the penult: *'chito,* "large," *fa'laia,* "long." *Atai* or *ạtai,* "buckeye," however, has end-stress. Moreover, a word that ends in a consonant takes the stress on the final syllable as a substitute for the verb "to be": thus *'hatak,* "man"; *ha'tak* "it is a man." In words of four or more syllables there is a secondary stress on the second syllable before the penult: *'hachun'chuba,* "alligator," *a'numpu'lechi,"* to annoy."

Elision of vowel and consonant is extremely common; so also is assimilation: *issi hakshup>issakshup;* "deerskin"; *yukpa>yuppa,* "glad."

Finally, it is of the utmost importance to note that the Choctaw adjective follows its noun, as in *nạni patạssa,* "a flat fish." The [ix] Creoles, by the way, have borrowed the adjective *patạssa* and use it in the sense of "perch." Compare Du Pratz, *Histoire,* II, 156 "Le Pattassa est ainsi nommé par le naturels, parce qu'il est plat ce qui signifie son nom: c'est le Gardon du pays," etc. In the southwestern part of Grant parish there is, too, a bayou by the name of *Patassa.*

I have given only such information about the Choctaw dialect as may be necessary for a clear comprehension of the sources of certain Louisiana place names. Further details may be found in Byington's *Choctaw Grammar,* Byington's *Dictionary of the Choctaw Language,* Gatschet's *Migration Legend,* pp. 116–118, and Bushnell's *The Choctaw of Bayou Lacomb, Louisiana.*

Besides the names of Choctaw origin there belongs to the Caddo dialect a small group of names, among which several are, unfortunately, of obscure or unknown meaning: see, for example, *Bistineau* and *Dorcheat, infra.* Furthermore, the Mobilian dialect has preserved at least one ancient name—*Plaquemine.* The Mobilian served as a medium of communication among all the tribes of the Gulf states. Based chiefly upon Choctaw, it had borrowed from many other Indian dialects. By the French it was called *Mobilienne,* from Mobile, the great trading post of the Gulf country; along the lower Mississippi it also went by the name of the Chickasaw trade jargon doubtless because of the striking resemblance between the Chickasaw and Choctaw languages.* The Atakapa dialect, in the next place, is represented by the strange name *Calcasieu* and most probably also by *Mermentau.* The word *Atakapa,* however, is itself derived from Choctaw *hatak,* "man," and *apa,* "eater," that is, "cannibal." In 1756 the present St. Martinville became officially known as the *Poste des Attakapas;* it was the seat both of the civil and of the military government of the vast Atakapa district. Old French inhabitants of St. Martinville may yet be heard to say, "Nous allons au Poste." The name *Atakapa* was formerly borne also by a county, which was created in 1804. The term *Atakapa* or Tukapaw country is not entirely obsolete.

Finally, a few names from other Indian dialects are found in Louisiana, but most of these names seem to have been imported at various times by white settlers.

---

* See Gatschet, I, 90 ff.; Mooney, in *B.A.E.,* 19th rep., pt. I, 187 (1898).

[x]BIBLIOGRAPHY WITH ABBREVIATIONS

The following publications have proved to be most helpful. Some others, of which but sparing use has been made, are cited in their proper places in the text.

American State Papers. Public Lands, Vols. I–VIII. 1832–34. G., ed., Green; G. & S., Gales & Seaton. Indian Affairs. Vols. I–II. 1832–34. *ASP*

Beauchamp, W.M. *Aboriginal Place Names of New York.* 1907, Beauchamp.

Bureau of American Ethnology. Reports, 1881 ff.; Bulletins, 1887 ff. *B.A.E.*

Byington, Cyrus. *Grammar of the Choctaw Language.* In *Proc. of the American Philosophical Society,* Vol. XI, No. 84. 1870. *Choc. Gr.*

———. *A Dictionary of the Choctaw Language.* Edited by John R. Swanton and Henry S. Halbert. 1915. *Choc. Dict.*

Charlevoix, Pierre de. *Histoire et Description Générale de la Nouvelle France.* Tomes I–III. 1744. Charlevoix

De Bow, J.D.B. *The Commercial Review of the South and West.* 1846–64; 1866–70. *De Bow*

des Lozières, Baudry. *Voyage à la Louisiane.* 1802. *Voy.*

———, *Second Voyage à la Louisiane.* 1803. *Second Voy.*

Du Pratz, le Page. *Histoire de la Louisiane.* Tomes I–III. 1758. *His.*

Fortier, Alcée. *Louisiana.* Vols. I–II. 1909. Fortier.

French, B. F. *Historical Collections of Louisiana.* 1846–53; 1869, 1875. French.

Gatschet, A. S. *A Migration Legend of the Creek Indians.* Vol. I. 1884. In Brinton's *Aboriginal American Literature.* Gatschet

Hodge, Fred W. *Handbook of American Indians.* Pt. I, Bureau of American Ethnology, Bull. 30, 1906; Pt II, ibid. 1910. Hodge

Maps by Darby, Ludlow, and others. Darby, etc.

Margry, Pierre. *Mémoires et Documents Originaux.* Tomes I–VI. 1875–86. Margry

Modern Language Notes. MLN

New Orleans *Times-Picayune. N.O.T.-Pic.*

Robin, C. C. *Voyages dans l'Interieur de la Louisiane.* Tomes I–III. 1807. *Voyages*

Shea, John G. *Discovery and Exploration of the Mississippi Valley.* 1852. *Dis.*

Spanish Surveys, *Lib.* VII, H and others, or *Book Z,* etc. Lib. VII, H, etc.

Swanton, John R. *B.A.E.*, Bulletins 43, 68, 73. Swanton

Thomassy, R. *Géologie Pratique de la Louisiane.* 1860. *Géol. Prat.*

Thwaites, R. G. *Early Western Travels.* Vols. I–XXXII. 1904. *EWT*

Walker, Norman McF. "The Geographical Nomenclature of Louisiana." In *The Magazine of American History,* Vol. X, pp. 211–222. 1883. Walker

Wilson, Harry D. *Louisiana.* Department of Agriculture and Immigration. 1925–26. Wilson

[xi] PHONETIC SYMBOLS

PHONETIC SYMBOLS

[g] go	[ɑ] or [ǫ] chop	[ɛ] bet
[hw] when	[ɑː] father	[e] chaotic
[s] say	[a̧] Choctaw hacha	[eː] pray
[z] zeal	[ɑu] cow	[ɪ] pit, city
[ʃ] shun	[ai] tie	[iː] see
[ʒ] pleasure	[a] French dame [ǫ] or [a] chop	[ɔː] saw
[θ] thin	[æ] hat	[oi] oil
[ð] that	[æː] there	[o] obey
[j] yes	[æ̃] a vowel inter-	[oː] low
[χ] loch	mediate be-	[v] full
[ŋ] song	[æ] and [ə]	[uː] moon
[r] red	[ɛ̃] French vin	[ʌ] sun
[l] Choctaw lipa		[ə] sofa
[tʃ] chin		[əː] bird
[dʒ] gem		

Other consonant symbols have their usual values.

     ' indicates strong stress on the following syllable.

     ` indicates secondary stress on the following syllable.

     ~ indicates a nasal vowel.

  > develops to.

  < develops from.

3. Phonetic symbols

[xii] THE ETYMOLOGY OF *BAYOU*

1719. "dans un bayou." La Harpe, in Margry, VI, 256.

The word *bayou* comes through French from the Choctaw *'bayuk,* "river," "creek," "bayou." In 1699 Pénicaut says: "A cinq lieues plus loin, en tournant tousjours à la gauche sur le lac, on trouve une eau dormante, que les Sauvages appellant Bayouque."[1] De l'Isle, Du Pratz, and Charlevoix use the form *Bayouc;* Ross has *Bayouc* (1765); Pittman, *Bayouk* (1770). By the opening of the nineteenth century the form *bayou* begins to establish itself both in French and in English, Duvallon (1803), as well as Brackenridge (1814), writing *bayou* with the plural *bayoux,* and Bradbury (1809–1811) referring to the Bayou Chiffalie.[2] During the first quarter of the nineteenth century the spelling *bayau* is of frequent occurrence, as, for instance, in William Darby's field notes of 1807–1808. But *Bayou,* one should observe, is not connected with French *boyau.* The Choctaw *'bayuk* is usually contracted to *bo:k* or *bo:g.*[3]

Various pronunciations of bayou prevail in Louisiana. In addition to the dictionary ['baiu:], one hears ['baiju:], remarkably often ['baio] or [baiə], and sometimes ['baijə]. In Creole French the usual pronunciation is [ba'ju], or, under the influence of rhythm, ['baju].

[1] ALPHABETICAL LIST OF PLACE NAMES

ABITA [ə'biːtə, æ'-] SPRINGS

1871. *Abeta Springs.* Hardee.
1873. *Abita; B. Abita.* Lockett.

The absence of early forms makes it difficult to interpret the name *Abita.* Bushnell thinks that it may have been derived from *Abiçka,* which was the name of an old upper Creek town, near Upper Coosa river, in Alabama. The Choctaw, he says, insist that *Abita* is not a Choctaw word; that an old man who called himself *Abeta* came from far away and made his home near the spring, so long ago that no Indian now living ever saw him. This man, Bushnell infers, may have been a Creek.[4]

If *Abita* is indeed a corruption of *Abiçka,* then one need only add here that the Creek word signified "pile at the base," or "heap at the root," a phrase which arose from the custom among the Creek warriors of covering the base of the war pole with a pile of scalps in contests for supremacy.[5] Observing, however, that the derivation of *Abita* from the Creek dialect rests chiefly on Choctaw tradition, I am tempted to seek another source for the word: so great an authority as Parkman declares that "nothing is more misleading than Indian tradition, which is of the least possible value as evidence."[6] The true source of *Abita* I take to be the Choctaw *Ibetạp,* which signifies "fountain," "source," "head, as of a water course." The etymology that I have suggested is supported not only by the environment at Abita Springs, but also by similar corruptions of *ibetạp* in the eighteenth century. On Romans's map of 1772 there are, to-wit, two Choctaw settlements, written respectively *Ebita poocola Skatane* and *Ebita poocola Chitto.* The first name is a poor spelling of Choctaw *ibetạp okla iskitini,* a phrase which signifies "small settlement at the fountain-head." The second name is meant for Choctaw *ibetạp okla chitto,* a phrase which signifies "large settlement at the fountain-head." Again, on the Purcell-Stuart map, which was [2] sketched not later than 1772, the same names appear, the one as *Ebitapoocolo Skalani* and the other as *Abitapoocolochitto.*[7] The conclusion seems to be well-nigh inevitable that *Abita* is nothing but a corruption of Choctaw *ibetạp.* The Choctaw word, let me add, would naturally lose its final consonant in Creole French.

Abita Springs is a village in St. Tammany parish, on the New Orleans Great Northern railroad, a few miles east of Covington. Abita has become a well-known summer and winter resort. The famous Abita spring is said to have a daily flow of almost 40,000 gallons. The town has about four hundred inhabitants, and was incorporated twenty-two years ago. The stream known as the Abita bayou or river joins the Bogue Falaya not far south of Covington.

ACADIA

The name *Acadia* originally designated territory that now comprises New Brunswick, Nova Scotia, and Prince Edward Island, besides parts of Quebec and Maine. Over this territory roamed the Micmacs, Malecites, and Abenakis—three tribes of the Algonquian race.

The origin of the name *Acadia* is obscure. Whether it is derived from the Micmac termination *acade*, "the place where something abounds," or from *acade* plus the classic name *Arcadia*, or from *Arcadia* alone, or from some other Indian or European word—no one has yet been able to ascertain. Eugène Rouillard has given a *résumé* of the various guesses as to the origin of the name.[8]

It is no part of my purpose to relate the story of the Acadian exiles. Here, however, are a few facts: During the year 1755 the British government deported over six thousand Acadians and drove many others to the wilderness. Of those who were deported a considerable number found their way to New York, Philadelphia, Maryland, Massachusetts, and other places. In 1765 more than six hundred arrive at New Orleans; later others came and settled along Bayou Têche, Bayou Lafourche, and the Mississippi. The settlements on the Mississippi, which were called the First and Second Acadian [3] Coasts, were situated just above the "German Coast," and extended on both sides of the river northward into Pointe Coupée. The German coast began about twenty-five miles up the river from New Orleans, and continued on both banks for about forty miles; it comprised, in other words, the area which since 1802 has been known by the name of the parishes of St. Charles and St. John the Baptist. As for the First Acadian coast, it is now included in St. James parish, which was created in 1807. Already in 1804 this coast had been officially designated as the County of Acadia; but after 1807 the home of the exiles from Canada did not receive recognition until 1886, when Acadia parish was created out of the southwestern part of St. Landry. Consult Fortier's *Louisiana*, I, 19–21; Wilson, pp. 143–146; Arthur G. Doughty's *The Canadian Exiles* (1921).

A station by the name of *Acadia* is situated on Morgan's Louisiana & Texas Railroad, in Lafourche parish, not far south of Thibodaux; Acadia is recorded on Cram's map of 1908.

ADOIS [ædi'o:s]

1816. *B. Adayes.* Darby.
1846. *B. Adois.* La T.
1873. *Adais.* Lockett.
1895. *B. Adias.* Hardee.

The Adai, a small tribe of the Caddo confederacy, formed one of the eight Caddo villages observed by Iberville on his journey up the Red River in 1699. Iberville called the tribe the *Natao.*[9] Long before his time, however, they had been mentioned by Cabeça de Vaca (1529), as the *Atayos.* In 1802 des Lozières estimated their number at one hundred men; eighteen years later they had dwindled to about thirty, who were living on Bayou Pierre, near Red River. These have lost their identity in that of other Caddoan tribes.

In 1715 settlements were established in the country of the Adai, by the Franciscans, and in 1716 there was founded in the same vicinity the mission of San Miguel de Linares. Furthermore, Broutin's map of 1722 has the words "Adayes Presidio Espagnol de la Province de Tecas,"[10] and marks the site of the post as distant "sept lieues [4] de chemin" to the southwest of Natchitoches. The Post of Adayes was evacuated in 1773 by its Spanish garrison, whose commandant at that time was Lieutenant Don Josef Gonzales. The old settlement of Adaize and the town into which it developed have long been extinct. They were near the site of the present town of Robeline, in the parish of Natchitoches.

The name *Adai* is derived from Caddo *hadai,* "brushwood," a term which doubtless referred to a conspicuous feature of the Adai territory. The Bayou Adois, which alone perpetuates the name of the tribe, flows about half a mile west of Robeline, and empties into Terre Blanc [Blanche] bayou. The local pronunciation of *Adois* as [ædi'o:s] results from an effort to imitate the sound of Spanish *adiós* [að'jos], with which the Indian name must easily have been confused by the early settlers.

ALABAMA

Alabama is the name of a bayou the main branch of which enters the Atchafalaya river, in the parish of St Martin. The name is derived from Choctaw *ạlba,* "vegetation," and *ạmo,* "gather"—in other words, "those who clear land for agricultural purposes."[11] The name does not mean, "Here we rest." Hodge, who gives nearly all the spellings of the name, records Bartram's *Alabama* (1791) as the earliest example of the modern form. This is also the spelling that was adopted by Ludlow in 1818, Graham-Tanner in 1834, La Tourrette in 1846, and Bayley in 1853; whereas the unique form *Albania* was recorded by Tanner in 1820 and again in 1839. La Tourrette, by the way, names the forks of the bayou—thus, "East Fork of B. Alabama" and "W. Fork of Alabama."

The Alabama bayou was named after the Alabama Indians, a prominent Muskoghean tribe whose home was originally on the Alabama river, not far below the junction of the Coosa and Tallapoosa rivers. When the French abandoned Fort Toulouse in 1763, they took with them into Louisiana a part of the Alabama tribe. Ross's map of 1765 shows the Alibamons as a settlement of only twenty men, on the east bank of the Mississippi, about sixty miles above New Orleans. It was here that Hutchins found them in 1784, as did also Bartram in 1777. In 1806 Sibley makes mention of a party of about [5] thirty Allibamis, who came to Red river and lived about sixteen miles above the "Bayau Rapide, until 1805, when most of them went up the river and settled near the Caddoques." For further information about the Alabama tribe, consult Hodge, I, 43 ff.; Gatschet, I, 88 ff.; Swanton, *Bull. 73, B.A.E.* (1922).

ALOHA

Aloha is the well-known Hawaiian word of many meanings—"love," "good morning," "good-bye," etc. About twenty-five years ago officials of the Louisiana Railway & Navigation Company are said to have selected the name for a village situated on their line, about seven miles northwest of Colfax, in Grant parish. The population is approximately 75.

ATCHAFALAYA [tʃæfə'laiə]

(a) 1718. *Chafalia.* De Lisle.
    1803. *Tchafalaya.* Duvallon, *Vue de la Colonie Espagnole, Carte* facing p. 1.
    1812. *Chaffalia. ASP,* I, 863.
(b) 1802. *R. Atchafa-Laya.* Robin.
    1816. *Atchafalaya Bay.* Darby.
    1817. *Atchafalaya.* Darby's *Louisiana,* 2d ed., page 125.

I have given but a few of the numerous spellings of *Atchafalaya.* These may be divided into two groups: (1) those that begin with "A"; and (2) those that begin without "A." The forms with initial "A" are the more primitive, though they do not occur as early as do some of the forms without the "A." The name signifies "long river"; it is derived from the Choctaw *hacha,* "river," and *falaia*, "long." The meaning of the name was not known even to so eminent a geologist as Thomassy, who remarks that *Atchafalaya* is generally thought to signify in the Indian dialect "grande eau"; but that William Darby declares, with much more "vraisemblance," the meaning to be "eau perdue."[12]

The pronunciation of *Atchafalaya* has long varied in accordance with the former variation in the spelling. In 1832 Timothy Flint asserted that the name was universally pronounced *Chaffalio*—a form [6] which of course signifies [tʃæfə'laiə].[13] Daniel Dennet, on the other hand, gave the pronunciation as At-chaf-a-lyre, to which one should doubtless assign the value of [æ't ʃæfə'laiə].[14] Nowadays the local pronunciation is strongly in favor of [tʃæfə'laiə]; but [ə'tʃæfə'laiə] and [æ'tʃæfə'laiə] are sometimes heard. Among those Louisianans, however, to whom the name is little more than a book-word, the usual pronunciation is either [ə'tʃæfə'laiə] or [æ'tʃæfə'laiə], the aphetic [tʃæfə'laiə] being seldom employed. The dictionary pronunciation ['ætʃəfə'laiə] is almost unknown in Louisiana, so far as I have been able to ascertain.

The Atchafalaya river leaves the Red eight miles by water from the confluence of the latter with the Mississippi, and flowing in a southeastward direction through that part of Louisiana which lies west of the Mississippi, finally enters the Gulf of Mexico. From Butte la Rose almost as far south as Morgan City, the Indian name gives way respectively to *Upper Grand* and *Grand River*. The Atchafalaya Bay is merely that part of the gulf into which the Atchafalaya empties.

A small post office by the name of *Atchafalaya* is situated on Morgan's Louisiana & Texas railroad, about thirteen miles northeast of Breaux Bridge, in the parish of St. Martin.

AVOYELLES [ə'voiəlz, æ-];[occ.avwa'el]

1758. *Avoyels.* Du Pratz, II, 241.
1767. *Avoyelles.* Morgan, in *Rep. 8th Int. Geog. Cong.*, 954 (1904).
Avoyelles probably means "*flint people*," or "*nation of the Rocks*." Iberville says in 1699 that a Tensas Indian applied the name *Tassenocougoula* to a stream which is now know as Red river.[15] In 1713 Pénicaut speaks of a nation called the *Tassenogoula*, a name which he interprets as the "nation of the rocks."[16] Furthermore, La Harpe calls the same tribe the *Tamoucougoula* or the *Anoy*.[17] If *Anoy* is a misprint for *Avoy*, and if, again, *Avoy* is short for *Avoyelles*, then [7] *Avoyelles* may have the same meaning as

Tassenocogoula, which is derived from Choctaw *Tasannuk* "flint" and *okla,* "people."[18] A less plausible etymology is that proposed by Gatschet, who sees in *Avoyelles* a diminutive of French *avoie,* "viper."

In the eighteenth century an Indian tribe by the name of Avoyelles lived near the mouth of Red river. They were probably a branch of the Natchez. By the beginning of the nineteenth century they had become extinct.

Avoyelles parish, which preserves the name of the Indian tribe, was organized in 1808. In 1830 the population of the parish was 3,484; in 1924, 35,793. In the parish there is also a bayou of the same name.

BAYOU BODCAU ['bɒdkɔ:]

Probably the earliest reference to the bayou now known as Bodcau is contained in an order of survey granted to Manuel O'Garte and signed by Governor Miro March 3, 1785. Here the name of the bayou is spelled *Batea.*[19] Unfortunately for the significance of this form, a *Requête* conceded July 18, 1799, by Commandant José Louis de la Bega, mentions the rivulet of *Bateria,* in the county of Natchitoches.[20] Furthermore, Sibley says in 1805 that the Indians called the lake *Badkah;* and Darby in 1816 makes use of the name *Bodcau.* The form *Bodeau,* which is found on the Graham-Tanner map of 1834, evidently arose through a printer's substitution of "e" for the "c" of the earlier *Bodcau.* Later still one comes upon such forms as *Badeau* and *Bodcaw.* The present spelling wavers between *Bodcau* and an occasional *Badcau* for the bayou; whereas *Bodcau* alone is used for the name of a small station on the Vicksburg, Shreveport & Pacific railway, in Bossier parish.

The spelling of proper names in the *American State Papers* is often so erratic and misleading that no conclusion as to the ultimate source of *Bodcau* may safely be drawn from the Spanish *Batea* or *Bateria.* Whether *Batea* or *Bateria* is due to a misapprehension of the Indian name, or was conferred on the bayou by the Spaniards in ignorance of the Indian name, is a question that may never be settled. It is [8] clear, in the next place, that *Bodcau* is older than *Bodeau,* the suggestion that the former may have arisen from the latter not being supported by the evidence from reputable maps and surveys.[21] But even if we accept *Badkah* or *Bodcau* as the primitive form, we are unhappily no nearer than ever to a knowledge of the meaning of the name. Here, as in the case of *Bistineau* and *Dorcheat,* we are baffled by the lack of a trustworthy Caddo vocabulary.

Bayou Bodcau, in Bossier parish, is merely a continuation of Bodcau river, which rises in southwestern Arkansas.

BAYOU BUSHLEY

1802. *B. Bachele.* Robin.
1813. *Bushley Cr. ASP,* II, 855, G. & S.
1816. *Bayou Bushley. ASP,* III, 212. D.G.

Bushley is taken from Choctaw *bashli,* a "cut," an "incision," a noun which is coined from the verb *bashli,* to "cut," to "saw." From the verb has also come the *nomen agentis bashli,* "cutter," "sawyer," as in *iti bashli,* a "sawyer,"—literally, a "woodcutter."

The two names that this stream bears are quite confusing. On some surveys it is called Bayou Bushley; on other, Bushley Creek; on others still, Bushley Creek, except for the last two miles above its mouth. The Indian name is highly appropriate; for Bayou Bushley is indeed a "cut-off," flowing in a southwesterly direction from the Ouachita, in Catahoula parish, and ultimately joining the stream that goes by name *Dry Fork.*[22]

BAYOU FUNNY LOUIS

1816. *B. Funné Louis.* Darby.
1816. *Bayou Funneleur. ASP,* III, 212. D.G.
1816. *Bayou Fenneleur, ASP,* III, 212. D.G.
1834. *B. Funne Louis.* G.-T.
1834. *B. Fanne Louis.* Illman.
1878. *B. Funny Louis.* Gray.

Derived from Choctaw *fani,* "squirrel," and *lusa,* "black," this name signifies "Black Squirrel" bayou. The translation "burnt [9] squirrel,"[23] as given by Kilpatrick and repeated by some later writers, is wrong. Folk etymology is responsible for the two forms ending in the French suffix *-eur.* Bayou Funny Louis is in La Salle parish, and flows towards the southwest into Little river.

BAYOU GOULA [baiə'gu:lə]; cf. *bayou, supra.*

Bayou Goula is derived, through the medium of French, from Choctaw *bayuk* and *okla,* "Bayou or River People." Compare Du Pratz's *Les Bayouc-Ogoulas.*[24] Bayou Goula, a town in Iberville parish, is situated on the Mississippi river and the Texas & Pacific railroad, nearly eight miles south of Plaquemine. The population of Bayou Goula is approximately 1,000.

The Bayogoula, a Muskhogean tribe, were living about 1700 at the town which bears their name; but by the middle of the eighteenth century the remnant of the Bayogoula had united with the Houma. Originally a red pole marked the boundary between the hunting grounds of the Bayogoula and those of the Houma; cf. *Istrouma, infra.* The little stream after which the Bayogoula were named empties into Grand river. On Ludlow's map of 1818 this stream is spelled *B. Gooler.* There seems to be no record of the exact time when white men occupied the site of the Bayogoula village; a census, however, of 1769 assigns the entire district of Iberville a population of but 376.

BAYOU LOUIS

1802. *Bayou Louis.* Robin.
1816. *B. Louis.* Darby.
Bayou Louis signifies "Black Bayou"; the name is derived from Choctaw *bayuk,* "bayou" or "creek," and *lusa,* "black." This bayou is on what is called Sicily Island, in the parish of Catahoula. Kilpatrick's translation of the name as "Squirrel Bayou" is wrong,[25] the Choctaw for squirrel being *fani.*

[10] BAYOU PLAQUEMINE BRULÉ

1816. *Plaquemine Brulé B.* Darby.
1853. *B. Plaquemine Brule.* Bayley.
1895 *B. Plaquemine Brulée.* Hardee.
On the origin and pronunciation of *Plaquemine,* see the word, *infra.* Some recent maps of Louisiana have dropped the word *Brulé,* "burnt," which referred to land that was cleared by the burning of cane and underbrush. By those who do not speak French, *Brûlé* is generally pronounced [*bru:lI*].

This bayou flows in a southwesterly direction, and empties into Bayou Cane, in Acadia parish.

BISTINEAU ['bistIno:]

I can make nothing out of this name. That it is of Caddo origin seems to be clearly indicated by Robin's form—*Bistiono.*[26] Such spellings as *Bastiano* and *Bestiano,* on the other hand, are misleading rather than helpful.[27] Virtually all that I can ascertain about the name is found in a remark made by James, who in his account of Long's expedition says that the lake is called "*Big Broth* by the Indians from the vast quantities of froth seen floating on its surface at high water."[28] On Ludlow's map of 1818 the name appears as "Bestino or Big Broth Lake." On Darby's map of 1816 the modern spelling is used. Darby gives an early and graphic account of this beautiful lake, which lies in the parishes of Webster and Bossier.[29]

BOGALUSA [bo:gə'lu:sə]

1803. *Arroyo negro ō Bog–holizà.* Pintado, in *Lib.* VII, H, p. 7.

1803. *"Bog-holizà,* Conocido por el nombre vulgar de *Black Creek."* Pintado, in *Lib.* VII, H. p. 11.

1818. *Bogue Luca.* Ludlow.

1846. *Bogue Loosa.* La Tourrette.

1825. *Bogue Lusa.* Rand.

[11] This name rests on the well-known Choctaw *bok* or *bog,* "creek," and *lusa,* "black." The stream used to be known, as old Spanish surveys state, by the name of "Black Creek." It flows though the town of Bogalusa, in Washington parish, and empties into Pearl river. Modern maps of Louisiana seem generally to record the spelling *Bogue Lusa* for the name of the creek and *Bogalusa* for that of the town; but the local pronunciation is said to be the same—namely [bo:gə'lu:sə]—for both. The stream is now called Bogalusa creek.

The view that *Bogalusa* may have arisen from an Italian laborer's exclamation "Broka-loosa" is too absurd to receive consideration in any serious study of place names.[30] The origin of the name is firmly established by the evidence of all the old forms.

The town of Bogalusa is situated on the main line of the New Orleans Great Northern railroad, seventy-two miles north of New Orleans. The town was of course named after the creek. Bogalusa has a commission form of government, which was created under special act No. 14 of the 1914 session of the legislature, dated June 11, and made effective July 4, 1914.

In 1906 the site of Bogalusa was a virgin forest of pine. The population is now about 18,000. Interesting data about Bogalusa are given in the New Orleans *Times-Picayune* for Tuesday, December 29, 1925, and especially in a pamphlet issued by the Great Southern Lumber Co., of Bogalusa.

BOGUE CHITTO ['bo:g'tʃItə]; sometimes ['bo:g'tʃItə]

1803. *Bogue Chitto.* Ellicott, *Journal,* map facing p. 202.

1804. *Barrio del Buck Chitto.* Trudeau, in *Lib.* VI, p. 26.

1816. *Bogue Chito.* Darby.

1818. *Bogue Chitto.* Ludlow.

Bogue Chitto signifies "Big River," being derived from Choctaw *Bok* or *Bog,* "bayou," "creek," or "river," and chitto, "big." The Bogue Chitto pursues a southwestern course through the parishes of Washington and St. Tammany, and empties ultimately into Pearl river.

[12] BOGUE FALAYA [bo:g fə'laiə]

1803. *Buck-falaya Arroyo.* Trudeau, in *Lib.* D., No. 4 G, p. 22.
1816. *Bogue Falaya R.* Darby.
1846. *B. Phalia.* La Tourrette.
1895. *Bogue Falaya.* Hardee.

The name of this stream is taken from Choctaw *bok* or *bog,* "bayou" or "river," and *falaia,* "long." The Bogue Falaya, or Long River, joins the Little Bogue Falaya just above Covington, in St. Tammany parish, and the current of the united stream swells the waters of the Tchefuncta.

BONFOUCA [bōfu'ka, -'ka]

Bonfouca was the name of a Choctaw chief who in 1747 made an attack with his band on the German Coast of Louisiana.[31] The name of the chief recurs in that of *Bayou Bonfouca,* a stream which joins the united waters of Bayous Paquet and Liberty in St. Tammany parish, a short distance north of Lake Pontchartrain. An early reference to Bayou Bonfouca is made by Pintado, in a survey dated November 5, 1807: "Entre los Arroyos vulgarmente llamados," he says, "el uno Bonfoucá y el otro de la Liberté."[32] Furthermore, des Lozières mentions in 1802 the *bonifoucas* among the savage tribes with whom he was familiar.[33]

I can suggest no satisfactory analysis of the first element of *Bonifoucas* or *Bonfouca.* Did *Bon*—or *Boni*—arise, through the error on the part of writer or printer, from Choctaw *bok,* "river," because of association with French *bon* or with the well-known form *Boni-,* as in *Boniface?* On the headwaters of Pearl river there was, at any rate, an ancient Choctaw village by the name of *Boukfouca,* as shown, for example, by the d'Anville map of 1732. By de Crenay, in 1733, the name is spelled *Boucffouca;* by Mitchell, in 1755, inaccurately *Bouefuka.* It is a significant fact that Carlos Trudeau, in a survey dated September 22, 1803, assigns to the present Bayou *Bonfouca* the name *Bucfuca.*[34] For the first element of the name one might think of yet another source—the Choctaw *abana,* "laid across, as [13] logs in a house,"—but for the fatal objection that the participle follows its noun in Choctaw.

The second element of *Bonfouca* is taken from Choctaw *fuka, foka,* "a place," "a residence." If then, Bonfouca is a corruption of *Bucfouca,* the original meaning must have been "river or bayou residence."

The river of Bonfouca is situated on Bayou Liberty, about four miles west of Salmens, in St. Tammany parish. Bonfouca forms almost the centre of an old French settlement, which within a radius of several miles has a population of approximately five hundred. Bonfouca station is on the New Orleans Great Northern railroad, four miles north of the village.

CABAHANNOSÉ

During the Spanish regime in Louisiana the present parish of St. James was generally called *Cabahannosé*. In 1766 a census was taken of both banks of the river from Dupart's to Hebert's places at Cabannoisé; in 1768 Nicolas Verret wrote a letter from Kabahannossé to Governor Ulloa; in 1777 Michel Cantrelle sent a message from Cabahannocer to Governor Galvez.[35] Again, Catahanose was named as one of the principal districts into which Spain had divided Louisiana; the parish of Catahanose, or first Acadian settlement, being said to have extended eight leagues on the river.[36] Here one may also add des Lozières's reference to Cabaanacé.[37]

The form with medial *t* is late and erroneous; the *b*-forms alone should be considered in any attempt at a solution of this peculiar name. The first part of *Cabahanossé* is obscure. Perhaps *Cahaba* is the Choctaw *kabaha*, "beater," "hammerer," which Dr. Swanton has suggested to me may have been used in the sense of "blacksmith." If this intepretation is correct— and it seems highly plausible—then the name would signify "blacksmiths sleep there," or "a blacksmith's shop"; for the second part of the name is unmistakably the Choctaw *anusi* or *anosi*, "to sleep there," a form which occurs in such compounds as *ofanusi*, "dog kennel," *pachanusi*, "pigeon roost," *shek(i)-anusi*, "buzzard roost."

[14] It was not until 1807 that the First Acadian Coast came to be known as St. James parish.

On maps of the first part of the nineteenth century there is shown a bayou by the name of *Cabanosé*. This bayou took its source from Bayou Lafourche, near Donaldsonville, and drained the angle between Bayou Lafourche and the Mississippi, finally losing itself in the lakes southwest of New Orleans. The name of the bayou is merely a syncopated form of *Cabahannosé*.

CADDO ['kædo:]

1687. *Cadodacchos.* Douay, in Shea, *Dis.*, 217.
    Cadodaquis. Joutel, in Margry, III, 411.

1701. *Cadodaquioux.* Pénicaut, in French, *His. Col.,* I, 73 (1869).
1716. *Cadojodacho.* Linarès, in Margry, VI, 217.
1743. *Kados.* Bruyère, in Margry, VI, 483.

The Caddoan confederacy consisted of about a dozen tribes, who formerly occupied eastern Texas, southern Arkansas, and the Red River Valley of Louisiana. The principal division of the confederacy was the *Kadohadacho,* which Gatschet translates chief tribe, from kado, "chief," "principal."[38] The form is sometimes given as *ka-ede.*

As early as 1542 Moscoso left the Caddo village of Nakado, which in the account given by the Gentlemen of Elvas is spelled Nondacao. In June, 1687, Joutel came to a village which he called *Cadodaquio* and in 1701 Indian guides conducted Pénicaut's party to the Cadodaquioux, whose village was situated about a hundred miles above the settlement of the Natchitoches Indians. The principal Caddo village, which was on a Caddo lake, bore the name of *Shachidini,* "Timber Hill." The survivors of the Caddoan family, now living in Oklahoma, are estimated with the Wichita, etc., at 1,226.

The name of the chief tribe has been given to Caddo parish and Caddo lake, as well as to hamlets in Louisiana. Caddo parish was organized in 1839, and was named by Mr. W. H. Spark. In 1925 its population was 96,171. Caddo lake, which is about twenty miles long, forms part of the boundary between Marion and Harrison counties, Texas; on the east it communicates with Sodo or Soda lake, [15] in Caddo parish, and thence ultimately with Red river.[39] The hamlet of Caddo is on the Kansas City Southern railroad, a short distance north of Oil City, in Caddo parish. Caddo Downs is a station on the Vicksburg, Shreveport & Pacific railroad, several miles southwest of Shreveport.

CAHOULA [kə'hu:1 ə]

Cahoula signifies "beloved water"; the source of the name is Choctaw *Oka,* "water" and *hullo,* "beloved." *Cahoula* is the name of a small creek that rises at St. Martinville, near the Bayou Têche, and flows into Catahoula lake, about nine miles to the northeast.

The local pronunciation, as Mr. J. A. Broussard, of St. Martinville, informs me, is not [kə'hu:1 ə], but ['ku:lI, 'ku:li]. The original pronunciation seems to have been replaced by that of *Coulée* or *Coolie,* a word used by natives in Southwest Louisiana in the sense of a small stream which during a part of the year often becomes entirely dry.

CALCASIEU ['kælkəʃu:]

Dr. Swanton writes me that this name is derived from Atakạpa *katkŏsh*, "eagle" and *yŏk*, "to cry." "Crying Eagle" was the war-title of an Atakạpa chief. Among some Louisianians the idea prevails that the name is a corruption of French *quelques choux*, "some cabbages"!

In the *American State Papers*, vols. II, III, IV, series of Public Lands, one comes across many curious spellings of the name—*Calcasuit, Culqueshoe, Culkeshoe, Kelke-chute, Quelqueshue*, etc. Darby writes it *Calcasu* 1816 and *Calcasiu* 1817; Ludlow, *Quelqueshoe* 1818; La Tourrette, *Calcasieu* 1846. A pronunciation current among old inhabitants of the parish is [kʌlkəʃui].

Calcasieu river, which has a length of about two hundred miles, flows in southwestern Louisiana through Lake Calcasieu into the Gulf of Mexico. The earliest reference that I have found to the river appears in Robin's *Voyages*, III, 14 (1807): "A dix lieues plus loin, dans l'ouest, est la rivière *Calkousiouk*. M. James Elliot, sous les ordres de don Joseph Pixnas, qui en a fait la découverte, assure qu'il n'y a pas de port plus avantageux," etc.

[16] The parish of Calcasieu was created in 1840, but out of its vast territory other parishes were subsequently formed. It contains 606,270 acres, and had in 1924 a population of 36,532.

Calcasieu, a station on the Gulf, Colorado and Santa Fe railroad, in Allen parish, is of comparatively recent origin.

CAMPTI ['kæmptI]

Campti is an old town, situated on the east bank of Red river, about nine miles north of Natchitoches. In 1805 Sibley says that the French had settled at Compti, the Indians having abandoned the village in 1792 on account of sickness. What was known as the Campti settlement embraced a considerable area lying north of the present site of the town. Campti was incorporated in 1903, and has a population of about 800. It is on the line of the Louisiana Railway & Navigation Company.

The town is said to perpetuate the name of an Indian chief who was known as *Campte*. He was probably of the Natchitoches tribe. I am not at all sure that his name is of Indian origin; it may be the French *Compté*. An examination of the early volumes of the *American State Papers*, in the Public Land series, shows that Indians went by such names as Baptiste, Bernard, Celestine, Louis, Pierre, Antoine, etc. An early spelling of the village name—Compté—apparently dates from the year 1788.[40] Other old forms are *Compti ASP,* I, 721, Ind. Affairs (1805), *Compte ASP,* III, 74, G. (1816), *Campte ASP,* II, 856, G. & S. (1812), *Campté,* Darby (1816). The modern spelling is found on the Graham-Tanner map of 1834.

CANNISNIA LAKE (De Soto parish)

1806. *Lac Pisaquié ou Canasenihan.* Lafon, *Carte Générale.*

The modern form of this name appears about 1832. *Cannisnia* seems to be the corruption of the name of an Apache tribe that once roamed over the territory far to the northwest of the present site of Natchitoches. Compare *Les Cannessy,* De l'Isle's map of 1718; *Les Canessi,* Bellin, 1744; *Canessis,* Robin, 1802; *Cannensis,* in French, *His. Coll.,* II, ii, fn. (1875); Hodge, I, 768–769, under *Lipan.*

[17] In 1700 Iberville estimated the distance from the Canessy to the Naouadiches at thirty-five or forty leagues[41]; in the same year Bienville said that a Nouadiche Indian used the name *Connessi* with reference to an establishment of negroes, situated at some distance from the Nouadiche village. Bienville interpreted *Connessi* with the words "les Noirs."[42]

CASTINE BAYOU ['kæstIn]

1699. *Castein Bayou.* Pénicaut, in French, I, 47 (1869).
   Castimbayouque. Pénicaut, in Margry, V, 387.
1705. *Castembayouque.* Pénicaut, in Margry, V, 459.
1758. *Castin Bayouc.* Du Pratz, *Histoire,* Map facing p. 139.
1834. *Bayou Castin.* Graham-Tanner.

The first element in this name is from Choctaw *kạshti,* "flea," and the second is from the Choctaw *bayuk,* "bayou." The bayou was so named because of the fleas that the Indians found on its banks. Cf. Bushnell, *The Choctaw of Bayou Lacomb,* p. 7.

On Louis Bringier's plan of Mandeville, Louisiana, drawn Jan. 14, 1834, this bayou is called "le petit Castaing." The bayou, which is at the east end of Mandeville, has been dredged at a cost of $30,000, and is now used as a harbor for boats drawing up to eight feet.

CATAHOULA [kætə'hu:1 ə]

1797. *Lago Cataoullou; Puesto de Ouachitta, ASP,* II, G. & S., *plano* facing p. 642.
   1802. *L. Kataouloup; Bayou Kataloloup.* Robin.
   1811. *Lake of Catahoula, ASP,* II, 685. G & S.
   1816. *Ocatahoola.* Darby.

1820. *Ocatahoola.* Tanner.

With regard to the origin of *Catahoula,* H. Bry says that Little River was called by the Indians *Etac-oulow,* or "River of the Great Spirit," which was subsequently distorted into *Cataoula,* the name of the parish through which the river runs.[43] Another translation is given by Dr. Kilpatrick, of Trinity, Louisiana, who says that the [18] name is taken from Choctaw *Ok-Katta-hoola,* "beautiful white water."[44] Yet a third analysis is that of Gatschet, who traces the word to Choctaw *okhạta,* "lake" plus *ougoula,* a French corruption of the Choctaw *okla,* "people."[45]

Of the three translations of Catahoula none seems to me to be quite satisfactory. Bry's form *Etac-oulow* is too corrupt for me to hazard a guess as to its origin, but Kilpatrick's is certainly meant for the Choctaw compound *oka,* "water,"—*hạta,* "white,"—*hullo,* "beloved." There remains Gatschet's etmology; this I am loth to reject, so great is my admiration of this eminent scholar's contributions to American ethnology. Nevertheless it is significant that those place names which contain the Choctaw *okla* betray their origin either by retention of a "k" or by a change of "k" to "g." A few examples are *Bayou Goula,* "Bayou people," *Pascagoula,* "Bread people," *Pensacola,* "Hair people." Two apparent exceptions are Iberville's *Pascaboula(s),*[46] and des Lozières's *Babayoulas.* But Iberville's form rests on a gross misunderstanding of the Indian source[47]; and *Babayoulas,* whatever its source may be, is hardly the same as *Bayagoulas.* The Babayoulas, says des Lozières, "habitent les hauteurs du Mississipi"[48]; the Bayagoulas, on the other hand, he placed "à onze lieues des tchactas, sur l'autre côté du fleuve."[49] Unless, then, a variant spelling with *k* or *g* can be discovered, the name *Catahoula* cannot be said to contain as its second element the Choctaw *okla,* "people."

I venture to suggest that Catahoula means "beloved lake"; that the name springs very clearly from Choctaw *okhạta,* "lake," and *hullo,* "beloved." The spellings with initial "O," though of later occurrence than some others, are actually the nearest of all to the Choctaw source. It is not without significance that Robin speaks of a very extensive lake named *Cataoulou,* which signifies, in the savage tongue, "'lieu de grand valeur.' Le Bayou prend lui-même aussi le nom de Bayou Cataoulou."[50] In view of Robin's statement and [19] the absence of *k* or *g* forms, I believe that Sibley, too, errs in thinking that Catahoula lake takes its name from that of an extinct Indian tribe.[51] The name of the lake, on the contrary, was conferred on the Indians who resided on its banks. Compare the origin of the tribal name *Okalousa.*

Catahoula lake, which is virtually an expansion of Little river, is about fifteen miles long, and varies in depth between fifteen feet and the shallow water of marsh land.

Catahoula parish was organized in 1808, during the territorial administration of Governor William Claiborne. It contains 440,000 acres, which are watered by the Red, Black, Ouachita, Tensas, Little, and Mississippi rivers, as well as by other small streams. It has vast timber resources. Its population is estimated at 11,345. Harrisonburg, the parish seat, is on the west bank of the Ouachita river, and has a population of about 400. The town perpetuates the name of John Harrison, a South Carolinian, who bought land on its site and had the town laid off in lots in 1818.

Besides the well-known lake and parish in the central part of the state there is, about nine miles northeast of St. Martinville, a small body of water also known as Catahoula lake. The French of that neighborhood pronounce the name *kata-'ula* or *kata-'ulu,* and Colonel Felix Voorhies of St. Martinville writes it *Cata-oullou.*[52] Finally, a bay by the name of *Catahoula* forms a part of the southern boundary of Lake Ouache or Salvador, in Lafourche parish. A bayou *"Cataollou,"* which, according to Ludlow's map of 1818, emptied into this bay, now connects a canal with the bay.

CATALPA [kə'tɔlpə; occ. kə'tælpə]

Catalpa is the name of a station on the Yazoo & Mississippi Valley railroad, two miles northeast of Bains, in the parish of West Feliciana. Catalpa is recorded on Cram's map of 1907.

Gerard derives *catalpa* from Creek *Kutuhlpa,* "winged head," a term used with reference to the blossoms of the catalpa tree. The Catalpa, or bean-tree, is common in Louisiana. More probably, the name is a corruption of *Catawba,* which has been traced to Choctaw *katapa,* "divided," "separated." *Catawba* was the name of a small [20] group of Indians who resided apart from the main body in South Carolina. See Hodge, I, 213.

CATAOUACHE ['kætə'wɔʃI, 'kætə'wɔʃI]

Until nearly the middle of the nineteenth century Lake Cataouache, in St. Charles parish, was called Duck Lake. In 1846, La Tourrette records the Indian name. Just south of Lake Cataouache, and indeed connected with it by two channels, lies Lake Ouache; see *Ouache, infra.* A prominent part of the shore line of Lake Ouache, one should next observe, is formed by Catahoula bay, which as early as 1820 appears on Tanner's map in the form *Cataollou.* It is therefore not unreasonable to assume that the comparatively modern name *Cataouache* results from a blend of *Catahoula* and

Ouache. Cata- is from Choctaw *okḥata,* "lake"; *Ouache* perpetuates a tribal name, but the meaning of the word has apparently been lost. Little or no significance can be attached, in my opinion, to the resemblance between *Ouache* and Choctaw *washa,* "a locust."

CHACAHOULA [tʃækə'hu:1 ə]

(a) 1816. *Chuckahoola B.* Darby.

    1873. *Chuckahoula; Chuckahoula B.* Lockett.

(b) 1830 & 1831. *Chichahowla* or *Cow Bayou.* T 16 S. R. 15 E. SE Dist. West of the river.

    1831. *Bayou Chickahoola.* Survey Traverse T 16 R. 15 E.

    1831. *Chickaloula* or *Cow Bayou.* T XVI R XV, E.

    1846. *Chickahoula* or *Cow Bayou.* La Tourrette.

(c) 1878. *Chacahoula Station.* Gray.

    1880. *Chacahoula.* Nicholson.

The forms of *Chacahoula* are arranged in three groups according to the vowel of the first syllable. The name is derived from Choctaw *chuka,* "home," and *hullo,* "beloved"—"beloved home." The second element of the name is also found in *Cahoula* and *Catahoula.*

Chacahoula is a village in the northern part of Terrebonne parish, about six miles southwest of Schriever. Pop., 1920: 334. The name is also applied to an extensive swamp in that vicinity.

[21] CHAPPEPEELA [tʃæpə'pi:1 ə]

    1846. *Chappapeela.* La Tourrette.

    1853. *Chappapela.* Bayley.

    1895. *Chappeau Pela River.* Hardee.

    1925. *Chappepela Cr.* Rand.

    1926. *Chappepeela Cr.* Map, La. Pub. Ser. Com.

Chappepeela signifies "Hurricane river," the name being clearly descended from Choctaw *ḥacha,* or "river," and *apeli,* "hurricane." *Hurricane,* one should observe, is a popular place-name in Louisiana and some other states. With the loss of the initial syllable of the Indian form, compare the evolution of such names as *Chinchuba* and *Tchefuncta;* with the word-order of the compound, compare that of Choctaw *peni luak,* "steamboat"—literally, *peni,* "boat" plus *luak,* "fire."

Chappepeela creek joins the Tangipahoa river about two miles north of Breckwoldt, in Tangipahoa parish. In this parish there used to be a village of the same name, as shown by the forms *Chapeau Pela* (Gray, 1878), *Chap-*

peau Pela (Nicholson, 1880), and *Chappeau Pela* (Hardee, 1895). There was likewise a *Bayou Chapeaupilier,* which the Graham-Tanner map of 1834 marks as a tributary of the Tickfaw river, in the parish of St. Helena.

Some of the later forms of *Chappepeela* are evidently due to confusion of the first element of French *chapeau.*

CHAUTAUQUA

Chatauqua is a station on the Chicago, Rock Island & Pacific railroad, two miles northwest of Ruston, in Lincoln parish.

Chautauqua is of course borrowed from the widely known name of the lake and village in the western part of New York. The origin of the name is obscure. Cornplanter, the Seneca chief who died in 1836, derives it from Mohawk *Jadáqua* or *Jadáqueh,* the "place where one was lost." A young squaw, it seems, once dug up and ate a root that created thirst; on drinking from Chautauqua lake, she disappeared. Hence arose the tradition that a root grows there which produces an easy death. Spafford, however, thinks that the word is a corruption of early Mohawk *Ots-ha-ta-ka,* "foggy place"; whereas Gatschet associates the word with Seneca *T'kantchata'kwan,* "one [22] who has taken out fish there," explaining his analysis by reference to the tradition that the Indians stocked Lake Erie with fish from Lake Chautauqua. Consult Beauchamp, pp. 38–40.

The Chautauqua systm of education was founded at Chautauqua village, under the auspices of Bishop Vincent of the Methodist church—the Chautauqua Assembly in 1874 and the Chautauqua Literary and Scientific Circle in 1878.

CHENANGO [ʃI'næŋ:o:]

Chenango is a station on the Texas & Pacific railroad, in the extreme southern part of West Baton Rouge parish. The name is an importation from the Seneca dialect, in which *Ochenango* or *Otsinango* signified "large bull thistles." The station is recorded on Cram's map of 1905.

Chenango is a well-known place-name in New York state. In the Ohio valley three distinct villages once bore this name. Some old spellings of the name are *Chenang, Cheningo, Cheningue, Ochenang, Zeninge,* etc.

CHICKAMAW BEND ['tʃIkəmɔ:]

Chickamaw Bend was the name of a curve on Pearl river, between Duckport and Milliken's Bend, on the eastern limit of Madison parish. The name is no longer used; but it is recorded on Lockett's maps of 1873 and 1882.

Chickamaw is undoubtedly corrupted from the Choctaw adjective *achukma,* "good." A similar corruption appears on Ludlow's map of 1818 and Graham-Tanner's of 1834. These show an Indian settlement by the name of *Yakunnee Chickama* in what is now Kemper county, Mississippi—a name that is clearly composed of Choctaw *yakni,* "land," and *achukma,* "good." The late appearance of the name in Louisiana points to borrowing from the Mississippi form.

CHICKASAW

The meaning of this name has been lost. Perhaps *Chickasaw* signified "rebellion," the term referring to the separation of the Chickasaws from the Creeks and the Choctaws.[53] The name has been [23] given to a creek in La Salle parish and to a station—Chickasaw Spur—on the Missouri Pacific railway, in West Carroll parish. A street in New Orleans also bears the name.

The important Muskhogean tribe of the Chickasaws once inhabited the northern part of Mississippi, their villages lying in the eighteenth century chiefly in Pontotoc and Union counties. Settlements of the tribe were also established on the Mississippi river, in West Tennessee, and in Kentucky. The present number of the Chickasaw nation in Oklahoma is 10,906. Consult Hodge, I, 260 ff.; Gatschet, I, 90 ff.

CHICKIMA

Chickima is a corruption of the Choctaw *achukma,* "good," Cf. *Chickamaw, supra.* Chickima is a plantation on the Texas & Pacific railroad, near Lecompte, in Rapides parish. Mr. P. C. Gariennie, of Lecompte, who spells the name "Chickama" and pronounces it ['tʃIkəma:], says that the name was chosen by a cousin of his about eighty years ago.

CHINCHUBA [tʃInt'tʃu:bə]

Chinchuba is a corruption of Choctaw *Hachunchuba,* "alligator." Chinchuba creek enters Lake Pontchartrain about two miles and a half west of Mandeville. The name of this stream was recorded by La Tourrette in 1846, and was given as "B. Chinchuba" by Hardee in 1871.

The village of Chinchuba is on the New Orleans Great Northern railroad, about three miles north of Mandeville, and about a quarter of a mile north of Chinchuba creek. In 1900 Chinchuba had a population of 75.

CHIPOLA [tʃI'po:1 ə]

The name *Chipola* at once suggests Choctaw *Chepulli,* "feast," "great dance."

Chipola is a small post office in the western part of St. Helena parish about 11 miles northwest of Greensburg. In 1880 Dr. E. O. Collins named it after Chipola in Florida. The present site of the post office is about a mile from that originally selected by Mr. Collins.

[24] CHOCTAW

The origin of the name *Choctaw* is unknown, the view that is perhaps a corruption of Spanish *chato,* "flat," having no support in the early accounts of the Choctaw tribe. Nevertheless it is true that the Choctaws formerly flattened the heads of their infants. Halbert thinks that the name may signify "separation," the term being used with reference to the ancient breach between the Choctaws and the Chickasaws.[54]

The powerful Muskhogean tribe that once inhabited the middle and southern parts of Mississippi has not bequeathed its name to any important places in Louisiana. The name, however, is popular enough, being found in the *Big Choctaw* and *Little Choctaw* bayou of Tensas parish, in the *Choctaw* bayou that enters Bayou Grosse Tête in Iberville parish, and finally in *Choctaw* and *Choctaw Pit,* two stations on the Texas & Pacific railway, in the parish of West Baton Rouge. In the last name the word *Pit* refers to a sand pit of about 25 acres, which was dug near the station during the construction of the Texas & Pacific road-bed.

The total number of the Choctaw nation was estimated in 1925 at 26,828.—Consult Gatschet, I, 100 ff.; Mooney, in *B.A.E.* Rep. 19. Pt. I, p. 500 (1898); Hodge, I, 288–289; Fortier, I, 539–562; *Rep. of the Com. of Ind. Affairs for* 1925. For the language see especially Byington's *Choctaw Grammar* and *Choctaw Dictionary.*

CHOUPIQUE

The Choctaw Dictionary defines *shupik* as the name of a fish called by some the mudfish. Whether the first syllable of this name is related to the Choctaw substantive *shua,* "stench," "filthiness," I am unable to say. The choupique frequents the bottoms of muddy, sluggish streams, and is considered inedible by most natives of Louisiana.[55] It is also known as the *bow-fin* or the *grindle*—dialectal *grinnel.*

The name *choupique* has been current in Louisiana for a long time. In 1699 Pénicaut describes a certain stream as follows: "A six lieues plus loin, il y tombe une petite rivière, que l'on nomme en sauvage Choupicatcha, les François la nomment aujourd'huy la [25] rivière d'Orléans, parce que depuis, comme nous le ferons voir en sa place, on a basti près de cette rivière, à une lieue de ce lac, la ville de la Nouvelle-Orléans."[56]

Subsequently Orleans river was called *Bayou St John*, in honor of Iberville's first name. It is not without interest to note that in 1719 Pénicaut uses the name *Bayou Choupic* instead of *Choupicatcha*.[57] Thirty-nine years later, on the other hand, Du Pratz distinguishes "Bayouc Tchoupic" from "un grand Bayouc, que l'on nomme le Bayouc S. Jean," placing the former at a distance of three leagues from the Pointe aux Herbes and the latter to the south of Lake Borgne.[58] However perplexing Du Pratz may be in one or two of his statements about the geography of this neighborhood, he is at any rate correct in his explanation of the origin of the name *Bayou Tchoupic:* "On nomme ainsi ce Bayouc, parce que l'on y pêche le poisson *Tchoupic*."[59]

As to Pénicaut's *Choupicatcha* a word of explanation may now be in place. This name is merely the Choctaw *shupik*, followed by *hącha*, "river." A similar formation is seen in *Taleatcha*, "Rock river,"—from Choctaw *tąli* and *hącha*. *Taleatcha* was the ancient Indian name of Pearl river. Pénicaut renders it incorrectly as the "River of Pearls," in French's version[60]; whereas in Margry's text he gives the misleading form *Tulcascha*, and nevertheless translates it correctly with the words "*Rivière aux pierres*."[61]

The following are some nineteenth-century spellings of the name *Choupique:*

1812. *Bayou Champique.* (County of Attackąpas.) *ASP,* I, 856. G. & S.

1825. *Bayou Show Pique. ASP,* IV, 72, G.

1825. *Bayou Chou Pique. ASP,* IV, 78, G.

1846. *B. Shupac.* La Tourrette.

1851. *Shore Pique.* De Bow, XI, 56.

1873. *B. Choupique.* Lockett.

[26] *Choupique* has various pronunciations. [ʃu'pik] seems to be preferred by those whose mother-tongue is French; ['ʃu:pIk] is often used by other Louisianians, while ['ʃu:peg] is not confined to the speech of the illiterate. The spelling *Shore Pique* points to yet another variation—perhaps ['ʃo:ə pi:k].

Choupique is a prosperous settlement of about thirty families, ten miles southwest of Sulphur, in Calcasieu parish. The settlement is nearly sixty years old. Not far away is Bayou Choupique, which empties into the Calcasieu river.

There is also a station by the name of Choupique on the Southern Pacific railroad, in the parish of St. Mary.

CHULA ['tʃuːlə]

Chula is Choctaw for "fox." It is the name of a station on the Texas & Pacific railroad, two miles from Tallien, in Assumption parish. The name is said to have been chosen, about 25 years ago, by officials of the railway company. A former Yazoo tribe was called *Chula*.

COLAPISSA [koːləˈpiːsə]

Colapissa, the 25th street north of St. Charles Avenue, in New Orleans, runs parallel with that avenue from Lowerline to Protection Street. Gatschet derives the name from Choctaw *Okla*, "people" and pisa, "see"—"those who look for people," that is to say, "sentinels" or "spies." Some French writers, however, take it from Choctaw *haklo*, "hear" and *pisa*, "see"—"those who hear and see."[62] In either case the name emphasizes the Indian custom of keeping an eye on persons who appeared near their settlements. The Acolapissa Indians resided first near the headwaters of Pearl river, then on the north side of Lake Pontchartrain, and later still—by 1722—on the east bank of the Mississippi, about thirteen leagues above New Orleans. Their identity has been lost in that of the Houma tribe. Some variant spellings of the name are *Colapissas,* Margry, V, 471; *Goulapissas,* de Lozières, 242 (1802); *Aquelou Pissas,* Nuttall (1818), in Thwaites' *Early Western Travels,* vol. 13, p. 357.

[27] COOCHIE ['kuːtʃI]

Coochie is a station on the Texas & Pacific railroad, about five miles south of Black Hawk, in Concordia parish. Hardee's maps of 1871 and 1895 prove that the name is shortened from *Withlacoochee* or *Withla Coochee.* The name has therefore not sprung from Choctaw *kŭsha,* "reed-brake," but has been corrupted from Creek *ui,* "water," *lako,* "great," and *uchi,* "little,"—"Little Great Water."

Withlacoochee is the name of a river and town in Florida; and in this state there was an old Seminole settlement by the same name. The Louisiana name was of course borrowed from that in Florida.

COOCHIE BRAKE

Coochie Brake is the name of a cypress swamp of more than 700 acres, lying between Verda and Atlanta, in Winn parish. Dunn says that the Spaniards built a fort at Coochie Brake before 1800.[63] *Coochie* is derived, I suppose, from Choctaw *kūsha(k)*, "reed," "reed-brake."

Near Grand Écore, not far west of Coochie Brake, there was a bayou by the name of *Coochenaha*, a bayou which was declared to be one of the boundaries of a tract of land claimed by the well-known John Sibley.[64] *Coochenaha* refers to a bayou from which the cane had been cut. The name is derived from *kūsha(k), supra,* and *naha,* "trimmed," "cut off."

COOSA ['ku:sə]

The hamlet of Coosa no longer appears on modern maps of Louisiana. Coosa was situated on Lake St. John, about three miles west of the Mississippi, in the extreme northeastern part of Concordia parish. It is recorded on Cram's map of 1907. On Lake St. John there is a plantation by the name of *Coosa,* as well as a bathing resort with the alluring title of "Cool Coosa Beach."

Coosa is corrupted from Choctaw *Kūsha,* "reed," "reed-brake." The name was aptly chosen: Dr. Kilpatrick said that the brakes were so thick in the vicinity of Lake St. John that one could hardly stick a bowie knife in them up to the hilt.[65] But *Coosa* was probably [28] borrowed from a similar place name in Alabama or Mississippi. The Coosa or Kusha Indians formed a group of the eastern Choctaw settlements in Lauderdale county, Mississippi.[66]

COUSHATTA [ku-,ku'ʃætə]

1853. *Cashatta Chute P.O.* Bayley.
1873. *Couchatta.* Lockett.
1878. *Coushatta Chute.* Gray.
1889. *Coushatta.* Century Atlas.

Coushatta signifies "white reed-brake"; it is derived from Choctaw *kūsha* or *kūshak,* "reed," "reed-brake," and *hᶏta,* "white." As the first vowel is nasalized in Choctaw *kūshak,* such a spelling as *Conchatta* is not uncommon, especially among early writers, as for example in Darby's *Bayou Conchatta.*[67] Lockett's map of 1882 records a *Conchatta Bluff* in Bossier parish.

The name *Coushatta* was originally applied to a band of Indians whose settlement was near a white reed-brake. Technically, the Coushatta are known as *Koasati*. During the second half of the eighteenth centry they inhabited the northern bank of the Alabama river, a few miles below the confluence of the Coosa and Talapoosa rivers. Coosada, in Elmore county, Alabama, is built on the same site. The Coushatta are a branch of the Muskhogean family.

Coming to Louisiana about 1795, they settled on Bayou Chicot and Red river; subsequently they spent some time on the Sabine river. In 1822 about 350 Coushatta were living on Red river. At present a village of approximately 60 Coushatta is situated about seven miles from Kinder, in Allen parish.

The name of the Indian tribe was given to Coushatta, the parish seat of Red river parish. Coushatta is on the east bank of Red river, on the line of the Louisiana Railway & Navigation Company. The town was incorporated on April 22, 1872. In 1920 it had a population of 962.

DORCHEAT [ˈdɔːtʃiːt]

This is a perplexing name. Long says that the Bayou Datche conducted his party to a beautiful lake called *Big Broth* [Bistineau][68] [29]. In 1805 Sibley mentions the Bayou Daichet.[69] Some other forms are:

1816. *Dacheet R.* Darby.
1818. *Bayou Datache.* Ludlow.
1846. *B. Dauchite.* La Tourrette.
1878. *B. Dorchite.* Gray.
1880. *Bayou Dorcheat.* Nicholson.

Such forms as *Dauchite* and *Dorcheat* result from an attempt to accommodate the spelling to the pronunciation of an original [aː] as [ɔː] in the first syllable. Though the origin of the name is not altogether clear,[70] I am strongly inclined to connect *Datche* with the second element of the name *Cadodaccho;* cf. *Caddo, supra.* Gatschet, if I understand him aright, takes this to be a general term for "clan," "people." *Datcho,* together with *Nadatcho,* is a tribal name of apparently similar origin.[71] The latter is identical with *Nadako,* the name of a Caddo tribe, which is in turn the same as the *Nondacao* of De Soto's expedition.[72] It is interesting to observe that Mooney translates Caddo *nadaka* by the phrase "with the people."[73] I conclude therefore that *Dorcheat* may signify "people" and thus perpetuate the name of some Caddo tribe.

Bayou Dorcheat rises in Arkansas and, flowing southward through

Webster parish, enters the northern end of Lake Bistineau. The hamlet of Dorcheat, spelled *Dachet* by Bayley in 1853, is in the northern part of the same parish.

FORDOCHE [fɔ:'do:ʃ:] occ. [fo:'do:ʃ]; rarely [fɛr'dɔ:ʃ].

> 1816. *B. Ferdoche.* Darby.
> 1846. *B. Fordoche.* La Tourrette.
> In 1807 Robin refers to this bayou as follows: "Les seuls bayoux Courtableau et Fordoches procurent aux habitans de ce district l'exportation par Plaquemine, de leurs dénrees à la Capitale."[74] Other streams in Louisiana have borne a similar name at various [30] times, but the changes in the spelling of the name are not marked enough to aid one in tracing its history. If it is Choctaw, it is very much disguised; for Choctaw has neither an "r" nor a "d." The Creoles of Pointe Coupée use *fordoches* in the sense of "trash," "rubbish," a usage which makes me suspect that the name may be a corruption of the French nautical term *fardage,* "dunnage." The bayou could easily have received its name by reason of the debris that obstructed its current. Fortier, however, remarks that the Creoles from the parish of St. Martin take the phrase "dans les Fordoches" to be synonymous with "dans la misère," "dans l'embarras." Unfortunately, the definition that he gives of *les Fordoches*—"remote settlement"—does not lessen the obscurity of the origin of the term.[75] On the other hand, Dunn, who thinks that the name is Indian, says that it signifies "lair for wild animals."[76] The fact, too, that a bayou in De Soto parish was once called *Fordache* seems to indicate a Caddo source for the name.[77] With respect to Bayou Courtableau, which is also mentioned by Robin, I should perhaps observe that it is named after a well-known French family; cf., for instance, the reference to Jacques Courtableau, in the *American State Papers,* II, 818. G. & S.
> Bayou Fordoche flows into Bayou Grosse Tête, in Pointe Coupée parish. There is also a village by the name of *Fordoche,* about twenty-five miles northwest of Baton Rouge. In 1920 Fordoche had a population of 226.

GENESEE

Genesee is derived from Iroquois *gen-nis-he-yo,* or *gen-nus-hee-o,* "beautiful valley," a term which was used with reference to the vicinity of Seneca towns near Fall Brook, New York, but which was also considered appropriate for the entire valley between Mount Morris and the rapids of South Rochester.[78]

The village of Genesee is situated on the Illinois Central railroad, about ten miles south of Amite, in Tangipahoa parish. It probably took its name from that of a county in New York. Twenty-five years [31] ago Captain Arthur Loranger, a Canadian by birth, left New York for Louisiana to become the president of the Genesee Lumber Company.

HOUMA ['hu:mə]; ['ho:mə]

The word *Houma* is taken from the Choctaw adjective *humma* or *homma*, "red." This term may have been used with reference either to the paint that the Houma warriors daubed on their bodies,[79] or to the color of their moccasins and leggings. A third possibility is that the name Houma represents an aphetic form of Choctaw *Shakchi humma*, or "red crawfish": the red crawfish is known to have been the war emblem of the Houma tribe.[80] The name is variously spelled—*Houma, Ouma, Homas, Omats, Oumats, Ommas.* See Hodge, I, 577.

The Houmas, a branch of the Muskoghean family, were living, at the close of the seventeenth century, in the northern part of what is now West Feliciana parish. At that time they were visited by Tonti, and a few years later they were encountered by Iberville. In 1699 their settlement contained 140 cabins and about 350 warriors. After a disastrous conflict with the Tunica in 1706 or 1709, the surviving Houmas settled on Bayou St. John, but moved within a few years to what is now called Ascension parish. D'Anville's map of 1732 shows a settlement of "Petits Houmas," several miles north of the mouth of Bayou Lafourche, and two other villages farther south, between the present sites of Donaldsonville and Convent. In his *Journal* of 1818–20 Nuttall writes of the Houmas as follows:

"Early this morning we passed the great plantation of General [Wade] Hampton, situated about 70 miles from New Orleans, at Ouma point, the name of a nation or tribe of Indians now nearly extinct, and who, with the remains of the Chetimashas, once living nearly opposite to bayou La Fourche, are at this time existing in a partly civilized state on the bayou Plaquemine."[81]

In 1836 Gallatin found a few Houmas in the vicinity of Manchac, on the east bank of the Mississippi.

The Houmas, mixed with the remains of other tribes, as well as with white and negro blood, now occupy the coasts of Terrebonne [32] and Lafource parishes. In 1907 they numbered, according to Swanton, from 876 to 890 souls. The time when they moved to their present settlements is not definitely known.

The name of the Indian tribe lives in that of Houma, a town which was founded by R. H. and James B. Grinage, and which in 1834 became the seat of justice in Terrebonne parish. Houma is situated on Bayou Terrebonne, just 52 miles from the Walnut Street ferry of New Orleans. The town is the center of the sugar cane section, and it is likewise famous for its crabs, shrimp, and oysters. It forms the terminus of a branch of the Southern Pacific railroad. The population of Houma is now over 7,000.[82]

The fact that the local pronunciation is often [ho:mə], by the side of [hu:mə], reminds one of the similar variation in the Indian source.

HURRICANE

Hurricane is an adoption of Spanish *huracán*, which in turn is derived from the Carib *huracan*. The Choctaw word for *hurricane* is *apeli*; c. *Chappepeela, supra.*

The hamlet of Hurricane is in Claiborne parish. There is a Hurricane creek in Caldwell parish, as well as a bayou of the same name in West Carroll.

ISTROUMA [Is'tru:mə]

Istrouma is a suburb on the northern boundary of the city of Baton Rouge. As applied to the suburb the name is quite modern; but as the ultimate source of the name *Baton Rouge, Istrouma* dates from the year 1700.[83] *Istrouma* is thought to be a corruption of Choctaw *iti humma*, which signifies "Red Pole"; and Baton Rouge is said to owe its name to the fact that on or near its present site the savages erected a painted pole, either in token of mourning or sacrifice, or—what is more probable—as a boundary mark between the territory of the Houmas and the Bayogoulas. Since *Baton Rouge*, however, is merely a translation and not a corruption of the Indian source, the [33] word should be discussed along with other place names of Romance origin in Louisiana.[84]

JATT or IATT [ʔaiət]

(a) 1811. *Bayou Jeat, ASP* II, plat facing p. 648.
    1818. *Lake Jet.* Ludlow.
    1853. *L. Jatt.* Bayley.
(b) 1816. *Lake De Yate. ASP,* III, 81.
(c) 1816. *Hietan L.* Darby.
    1820. *Hietan Cr.* Tanner.
(d) 1846. *Lake Iatt.* La T.
    Darby's name for the lake—*Hietan*—furnishes the clue to the source of the name, which La Tourrette's spelling—*Iatt*—points to the present pro-

nunciation. The Indians of the plains were accustomed to designate the Ute Indians by the term *Yuta,* whence have come *Eutaw, Utah,* and *Ute. Yuta* became in the Kiowa dialect *Iata(go),* which in turn was nasalized by the Sioux. From the nasalized form the early French explorers and traders got such forms as *Iatan, Ietan, l'Iatan, Ayutan,* and *Hietans.* Some of these forms were easily misread as *Jatan, Jetan,* and even as *Tetau.* Finally, *Jatan* was shortened to *Jatt,* and *Iatan* to *Iatt.* Spellings with initial *Y* evidently rest on an obsolete pronunciation. Unfortunately, the meaning of the name has been lost. See Mooney, in *B.A.E.* Rep. 17, 167 (1896).

Hietans, it is now important to observe, was another name for the southern Comanche. In 1850 this tribe numbered about 10,000 souls. They were constantly on the move; and their range extended from the Red river to the Colorado. They were fine horsemen, and lived by hunting the buffalo, which they killed with the spear. Their tents were made of buffalo skins, shaped like cones, and large enough to accommodate fifty or sixty persons. The Hietans have been reduced to 1,718, who reside on the Kiowa reservation, in Oklahoma. See Long, in *Early Western Travels,* XVI, 122, and Gregg, *ibid.,* XX, 120 ff.

Lake Iatt is in the northwestern part of Grant parish.

Big Iatt creek rises in Winn parish and flows into this lake. Northeast of the lake there is also a village that bears the name *Iatt.*

[34] KEATCHIE ['ki:tʃI]

The town of Keatchie is situated on the Houston & Shreveport railroad, about eighteen miles northwest of Mansfield, the capital of De Soto parish. The Baptists organized a church at Keatchie in 1852 and a college in 1857. Bayley in 1853 has *Kechi P.O.;* Lockett in 1873 uses the form *Keatchie;* some modern maps prefer *Keachie.* In 1920 the population was 516.

Keachie was named either after an Indian or after a small tribe of Caddoan stock. In either case the meaning of the word is the same, for the Caddoan *Kishi* signifies "panther."

At the beginning of the eighteenth century the Kichai were living on the upper reaches of Red river, in Louisiana. For the further history of the tribe, consult Hodge I, 683; Powell, *B.A.E.,* Rep. 14, Part 2, 1092 ff.

KISATCHIE [kI'sætʃI]

1811. *Bayou Casatches. ASP,* II, 713. D.G.
       Bayou Quisaschie. ASP, II, 712. D.G.

1846. *B. Casatche.* La Tourrette.

1873. *Kisatchie B.* Lockett.

The name *Kisatchie* seems to be derived from Choctaw *kŭsha(k),* "reed," "reed-brake," and *hącha,* "river." The first element also appears in *Kusa, Coosa,* or *Cusha,* which was the name of eastern Choctaw settlements on the Cusha creeks, in Lauderdale county, Mississippi.[85]

Kisatchie is the name of a creek or bayou in the southern part of Natchitoches parish. About three quarters of a mile north of the bayou there is a post office by the same name; the latter appears on Nicholson's map of 1880.

LATENACHE or LATINACHE ['lætInæ:ʃ]

(a) 1812. *Bayou Atenache. ASP,* II, 328. Green.

    1830. *Bayou Latenache.* T. III, R. VII E. SW Dist.of Louisiana.

(b) 1816. *Bayou Latania.* Darby.

    1818. *B. Lattanier.* Ludlow.

(c) 1834. *B. Lananacha.* Graham-T.

[35] That this is an Indian name is by no means certain; for the *b*-forms may be the earliest. If *Latania* is the original name, it must have been corrupted into *Latenache* under the influence of *Fordoche,* the name of neighboring bayou. *Latania* is a latinized form, to which corresponds the French *Latanier,* "fan palmetto." This species of palmetto is common in Louisiana.

If *Latenache,* on the other hand, is the earlier name, I can only guess at its etymology. The Choctaw substantive *ʃatimo* signifies "mire," "bog"; and *ʃatimo,* if followed by Choctaw *hącha,* "river," might easily be contracted to *Latemacha.* One would next have to ascribe the *n* in *Latenache* either to a printer's error or to assimilation because of the preceding *t.* The view that the *n* may have arisen from an original *m* is supported by one of H. S. Tanner's early maps, on which the name of the bayou is recorded as the *Lacamacha* river. Taking the first *c* as a misprint for *t,* one would actually have *Latamacha,* "bog(gy) river."

Bayou Latenache is in Pointe Coupée parish.

LITTLE BOGUE FALAYA ['litlboːgfə'laiə]

Pequeño Bog falaya. Plat in Pintado's hand, drawn probably between 1803 and 1808. *Book Z,* p. 85.

1821. *Bayou Little Bogue Falaya.* T.6 S, R. II, E. Greensburg Dist., La.

1846. *Lit. B. Phalia.* La Tourrette.

1895. *Little B.* Falaya. Hardee.

Little Bogue Falaya signifies "Little Long Creek" or "Little Long Bayou." For the derivation see that of Bogue Falaya, *supra.* These two streams unite north of Covington, in St. Tammany parish.

MANCHAC ['mænʃæk]

1699. *Manchaque.* Pénicaut, in Margry, V, 386.
1712. *Manchacq.* Pénicaut, in Margry, V, 497.
1713. *Manchac.* Pénicaut, in Margry, V, 508.

According to French's version, I, 46 (1869), Pénicaut writes in 1699: "We continued our way, along the borders of *Lake Pontchartrain*, in order to make the circuit of it, and, at the distance [36] of about five leagues further on, encamped on the borders of a *manchac*, which signifies, in the French language, a strait, a pass, or a rivulet, flowing from the *Mississippi.*"

Though Pénicaut gives the correct definition of *Manchac*, he fails to state the actual source of the word. Perhaps it springs, as Dr. Swanton has suggested to me, from Mobilian or Choctaw *imashaka*, "rear," or probably "rear entrance," with nasalization of the second syllable. Cf. Choctaw *âshaka*, prep., "behind," "in the rear."

During the eighteenth century Bayou Manchac formed an important waterway, flowing out of the Mississippi about fourteen miles by river below Baton Rouge and connecting with the Amite river, thence with Lake Maurepas, and ultimately with Lake Pontchartrain. General Andrew Jackson, fearing that the English might cut him off in the rear by effecting an entry into the Mississippi through Lake Pontchartrain and Bayou Manchac, had the bayou filled in 1814 at what is now the station of Rhodes, distant ten miles below Baton Rouge by the Yazoo & Mississippi Valley railway. Students of history will also recall that Fort Bute, which was taken by Galvez in 1779 from its British garrison, was built on the upper side of Bayou Manchac, at the point where the bayou joins the river.[86]

Bayou Manchac must not be confused with the comparatively modern hamlet of Manchac (P. O. name *Akers*), situated on the Illinois Central railroad, in the southern part of Tangipahoa parish. The hamlet is recorded on Lockett's map of 1873. The bayou passes Hope Villa, nearly 14 miles southeast of Baton Rouge, and enters the Amite river several miles north of Port Vincent, in Livingston parish.

An earlier Indian name of Bayou Manchac was *Ascantia*,[87] which seems to be a contraction of Choctaw *oski* "cane," "canebrake," and *āsha*, "is there."

For a time the bayou also bore the name of *Iberville* river.[88] The channels between Lakes Maurepas and Pontchartrain are still called *Pass Manchac*.

MARINGOUIN [marɛ̧ʼ:wɛ̧]

Maringouin is the name of a bayou and a town in Iberville parish. For more than two hundred years the French of Louisiana have [37] used *Maringouin* to designate a swamp mosquito. *Maringouin* is said to have been corrupted from *Marigoui,* a word found in some Indian dialects of Brazil. On Robin's map of 1802 the bayou is called *R. Maringoin.* In 1920 the town, which is of comparatively recent origin, had a population of 399.

MERMENTAU [ʼmə:mɛntɔ], [ʼməmintɔ:], [ʼmə:məntɔ:]

In the last quarter of the eighteenth century there was an Atakapa chief by the name of Nementou. On April 16, 1784, he is known to have executed, in favor of Antoine Blanc, a deed of sale to a tract of land on the Bayou Plaquemine Brulé;[89] and subsequently he is mentioned as the chief of the village on the river of the same name.[90] Again, a deed of sale, dated July 4, 1786, defines the boundaries of a tract of land by reference to the banks of the river Nementou.[91] Finally, another deed of sale was executed in 1802 by three Indians, among whom was Celestin, a chief of the Atakapa Indians of Nementou.[92] The history of the name *Mermentau* now seems clear: *Nementou,* the name of an Atakapa chief, was given to the river on which his village had been established. Compare the phrase "on the river and lake of Nementou," in a deed of December 10, 1803.[93] Through a clerical error *Nementou* became *Mementou,* and the latter was in turn corrupted by folk etymology into Mermentau through confusion with French *mer,* "sea." The modern spelling *Mermentau* is used by Darby in 1816; and as early as 1805 reference is made by Ceballos to the river under the name of *Armenta* or *Marmentoa.*[94]

Some other obsolete spellings, among which those of the aphetic type are noteworthy, are the following for the name of the river:

1811. *Nementoa.* ASP, II, 807. G. & S.

1820. *Mermenton.* Tanner.

1846. *Mermentou.* La Tourrette.

1814. *Mentou.* Brackenridge, *Views of Louisiana,* 171.

[38] 1834. *Mentao.* Graham-Tanner.

1838. *Mermentan* or *Menton.* Chapin, *Gazetteer,* 181.

1859. *Mentaur.* De Bow, XXVI, 602.

The development of *Mermentau* from *Nementou* is not in accord with a suggestion made by Thomassy. On Robin's map of 1802 the Mermentau river is shown under the name of R. *du [de] Lobos ou Mementao*. Thomassy thinks that *Lobos* means "sea-cows,"[95] and that *Mementao* is perhaps a corruption of *Lamentaou*, a dialectal form of French *Lamentin* or *Lamantin*, "sea-cow." Robin's *Mementao*, in other words, is merely a translation of *Lobos Marinos*, and has its ultimate source in the Carib *Manattoui*, "sea-cow." Compare the Spanish *manati* or *manato*, whence has sprung English *manatee*. If Thomassy's analysis is correct, the name of the Indian chief and that of his village are adopted from the name of the river.

To accept Thomassy's analysis one would have to assume that Robin either overlooked a serious printer's error, or had no knowledge of the word *lamantin*, and that Ceballos, too, was not familiar with Spanish *manati*. Else why did the Spaniard call the river the *Armenta* or *Marmentoa?* It is, moreover, significant that Robin, though recording on his map two names for more than one river, does not give unmistakable synonyms for a single stream. I conclude that the *Mermentau* was originally named *Nementou* after the Atakapa chief and his village, which was situated on the west side of the river. Unfortunately, the meaning of the name *Nementou* has been lost, though Gatschet, Dr. Swanton writes me, records *Inmantu-a* as the original Atakapa form.

The Mermentau river is formed by the united streams of Bayous Nez Piqué, Plaquemine Brûlé, and Queue de Tortue. It forms a part of the boundary between the parishes of Acadia and Jefferson Davis, and flows through Cameron parish into the Gulf of Mexico.

Mermentau is a village in Acadia parish, on the Southern Pacific railroad five miles east of Jennings. In 1920 the population of Mermentau was 364. The spelling *Mermenton* for the name of the post office is obsolete.

Mermentau Prairie lies between Bayous Plaquemine Brûlé and Queue de Tortue.

[39] MISSISSIPPI

The name *Mississippi* is derived from Algonquian *misi*, "great," and *sipi*, "water." Other translations are misleading, notably that of Du Pratz, who, using the form *Meact-Chassipi*, declares its meaning to be literally "vieux Père des Rivières."[96] First heard by the early French missionaries and explorers from the lips of the Indians who lived on the upper reaches of the Mississippi, the name came gradually to include the entire course of the river. Thus it displaced other names, such as *Rio Grande, Buade, Rivière de la Conception, Colbert,* and *St. Louis.* The first European to use the common Indian name was Peñolosa, the governor of New Mexico, who in 1661 wrote it *Mischipi.* Father Allouez's spelling in 1667 was *Messipi;* Marquette's in 1673, *Missisipi.* The modern spelling occurs as early as 1718, but it was not adopted exclusively until the nineteenth century.[97]

The Mississippi has borne many other names.[98] Among the Indian names of the river one of the most interesting is *Malbanchya* or *Malbanchia*[99]— less accurately, in French's translation, *Malabouchia.*[100] Compare, further, Coxe's *Malabanchia,* Du Pratz's *Balbancha,* and Dumont's *Barbancha.*[101] The Indian name is obviously the Choctaw substantive *Bạlbancha,* "a place for foreign languages," which is composed of *bạlbaha,* "one that speaks a foreign language," and the verb *âsha,* "be there." It should be mentioned here that the Choctaw *m* is not infrequently substituted for *b* as in *maleli* by the side of *baleli,* "to run." The name was applied first to the lower Mississippi and then to the city of New Orleans, the Indians looking upon the river and the city alike as places where foreign languages were spoken. Purely of Indian origin, the name has nothing whatever to do with the French words *male bouche,* with which it has been confused by some writers on the early history of Louisiana. *Bạlbancha* or *Mạlbancha* is no more akin to *male bouche* [40] than is the name of the creek *Chappepeela* to French *chapeau, supra.* Here one may be interested in learning that the imagination of the Indian shows itself in the Choctaw term for the mockingbird— *hushi bạlbaha,* "a bird that speaks foreign tongues."

The main facts with regard to the discovery and geography of the Mississippi river are too well known to require repetition in this paper.

NATALBANY ['tɔːlbənɪ; næt'ɔːlbənɪ]

1732. *Nitabani ou R^{ue} de l'ours.* Danville.
1765. *Nitabani or Bear R.* Ross.
1768. *Natabani or Bears R.* Jeffereys.
1794. *Nita Albany.* Laurie and Whittle, Map.
1816. *Notalbany R.* Darby.
1846. *Natalbany Cr.* La T.
1878. *Natalbany R.* Gray.

The name *Natalbany,* to judge from the earliest forms, springs from Choctaw *nita,* "bear," (ursus) and perhaps the adjective *bano,* "mere," "only," the Natalbany river having been undoubtedly a favorite haunt of the bear. Compare Choctaw *foni,* "bone" and *bano,* a combination which is translated "bony," "full of bones." *Natalbany* may signify "Lone Bear."

The second element, however, is nearer in form to the Choctaw *abani,* "a curer," "one who cures meat over a fire," a noun which is taken from the verb *abani,* "to barbecue." That this latter analysis is not unreasonable appears from the frequent references to barbecued bear meat—"de l'ours boucané"—in the works of the early explorers.[102]

Romans, on the other hand, refers to the character of the country "west from Mobile bay to Nita Albany, or Bean-Camp, at Lake Maurepas."[103] He wrote, or intended to write, *Bear-Camp,* the *n* in *Bean-* being a clerical error for *r;* but he erred in rendering the second element of the name literally by the word *camp,* inasmuch as the Choctaw for *camp* is *abina,* whereas the earliest spellings uniformly have *bani* as the second element. His translation, indeed, [41] is not far wrong; some well-known curer of bear meat, I think, must have built a hut or camp on the bank of the Natalbany river.

The substitution of a known for an unknown element, as *Albany* for *bani,* is common in the evolution of place names.

The local pronunciation of *Natalbany,* I am informed by my friend Mr. Cecil Bird, is [tɔːlbənɪ]. Brackenridge's spellings *Talbany* and *Talbana* prove that this pronunciation is over a hundred years old.[104]

The Natalbany river, with its headwaters partly in St. Helena and partly in Tangipahoa, flows southward through western Tangipahoa and a part of Livingston parish, and joins the Tickfaw a few miles above the point where the latter falls into Lake Maurepas.

The town of Natalbany is situated 4 miles north of Hammond, in Tangipahoa parish, at the junction of the Illinois Central and the New Orleans, Natalbany & Natchez railroads. In 1920 the population was 225.

NATCHEZ

The dialect of the Natchez Indians is Muskhogean; but the origin of the tribal name is unknown. Gatschet, indeed, would derive it either from Chetimacha *naksh asi,* "hurrying man," "warrior," or from Mobilian *naksika,* "away from," the latter interpretation having reference to the distance of the ancient Natchez villages from the Mississippi river. Swanton can find no basis for either etymology.[105] The Natchez are now virtually extinct. For early variants of *Natchez,* see Hodge, II, 36; and for the history of the tribe, consult Swanton, *B.A.E.,* Bull, 43.

Natchez is a station on the Texas & Pacific railroad, about six miles south of Natchitoches. Pop. 1920: about 150. The name of the Indian tribe is also borne by several bodies of water—by a small lake in the northwestern part of Grant parish, by a bayou that crosses the boundaries of

Winn and Grant parishes, and finally by a bayou and a lake or bay in the southern part of Iberville parish.

Lake Natchez, in Grant parish, was formerly called *Nantaches* [næn'tætʃI]; *Nantaches*, indeed, is the sole name by which it is locally known today. In 1846 La Tourrette called it *Lake Natchez*; [42] but already in 1816 reference had been made to *Lake Nantaché*.[106] During the nineteenth century, the name was usually written *Nantaches*; cf. Lockett, 1873, 1882; Hardee, 1895. *Nantaqui Lake* is the form given on one of Tanner's early maps. In the opening years, however, of the twentieth century the name *Natchez* reappeared, as, for instance, on Cram's map of 1905.

Nantaches is undoubtedly a variation of *Nataché*, the name given by Iberville's Indian guide in 1699 to a small Caddo village on Red river.[107] Gatschet does not translate *Nataché*; but Hodge thinks that the name may refer to a subdivision of the *Nabedache*. *Nabedache* signifies "a fruit resembling the blackberry"; but the earlier name of this Caddo tribe was *Nawadishe*, "salt," a name which indicates that the tribe lived near a supply of salt.[108]

NATCHITOCHES ['nækItoʃ]

1690. *Nachitoches*. Tonti, in French, I, 72 (1846).

1700. *deux cabanes de Natchitoches*. Iberville, in Margry, IV, 437.

1715. *un fort aux Nassitoches*. Pénicaut, in Margry, V. 537.

1721. *au fort de Saint-Jean-Baptiste de Naquitoche*. Belle-Isle, in Margry, VI, 341; *ibid., aux Naquitoches*.

1753. *Fort Naquitoches*. Dumont, in French, V, 33.

There are several translations of the name *Natchitoches;* "chinquapin eaters," "chestnut eaters," and "pawpaw eaters" are three that I recall. The Caddo form is *Nashitosh*; and according to information kindly furnished me by Dr. Swanton, it signifies "paw-paws."

Though the form *Natchitoches* alone survives, the local pronunciation, based on *Naquitoches*, is usually ['nækItaʃ] or ['nækItoʃ]. In rapid speech the vowel of the last syllable may be weakened almost to [ə]. A dictionary pronunciation ['nætʃI'totʃIz] is never used by natives of Louisiana.

The Natchitoches were a Caddoan tribe that inhabited the vicinity of the present town of Natchitoches, the capital of Natchitoches parish. See Hodge, II, 37.

[43] Natchitoches, the oldest town in Louisiana, is situated on the Cane river and the Texas & Pacific railroad, about seventy-miles southeast of Shreveport. The town was incorporated on July 5, 1872; in 1924 it had a

population of 3,696. The parish of Natchitoches contains 825,600 acres, and in 1924 had a population of 39,707. See Fortier II, 206 ff.; Wilson, pp. 189–190.

About November 1, 1714, Governor Cadillac despatched Louis Juchereau de Saint Denis on an expedition to the Natchitoches Indians as well as to the Spaniards of Mexico. With the Indian tribe the French, it should be noted, had already been trading for about fourteen years. After leaving ten men in charge of certain merchandize that he stored in the village of Natchitoches, Saint Denis continued his journey to Mexico. There he met and married Maria, the daughter of Don Pedro de Vilesca. Saint Denis then returned to make his report to Cadillac. On learning that the French need not hope to establish trade relations with the Spanish, Cadillac instructed Bienville, who was then at Natchez, to build a fort among the Natchitoches; and, in order to carry out the Governor's wishes, Bienville selected a veteran officer by the name of de Tissenet, who with the aid of the Natchitoches themselves built a fort in 1715 within a remarkably short time. The fort was erected on the bank of Red river, but was removed in 1721 to high ground, about a hundred yards west of its original site. On December 2, 1721, Saint Denis was appointed commandant of the fort. Such seem to be the essential facts with respect to the early settlement of Natchitoches.[109]

According, however, to French's version of the Pénicaut narrative, Saint Denis arrived at the village of the Natchitoches as early as 1713. There he remained for six weeks. During that time he had his men build two houses in the village for the storage of needed supplies, which he entrusted to the care of ten French soldiers. He then resumed his journey to Mexico.[110]

NOTTOWAY

Nottoway is a station on the Texas & Pacific railroad, several miles northwest of White Castle, in Iberville parish.

[44] Nottoway is an English corruption of *nadowa*, "rattle-snakes," a term which was applied by the Algonquian tribes to an Iroquoian tribe of southeast Virginia. As late as 1825 there resided in Southampton county, Virginia, forty-seven survivors of this tribe with their queen. A county, a courthouse, and a river perpetuate the tribal name in Virginia.[111]

The Nottoway plantation in Louisiana was named in 1858 by Mr. John Hampden Randolph, after the county in Virginia from which his father Peter had come.[112]

OKALOOSA [oːkəˈluːsə]

Okaloosa signifies "black water"; the name is from Choctaw *oka,* "water" and *lusa,* "black." A small Indian tribe by this name once lived west and north of Pointe Coupée.[113] The name is perpetuated by that of a rural high school and small community, situated about twelve miles southwest of Monroe, in Ouachita parish. *Okaloosa* is recorded on Gray's map of 1878.

OPELOUSAS [ǫpəˈluːsəs]

The origin of this name is not altogether clear. The first element may be from Choctaw *ąba,* "above," or from Choctaw *ąpi* "trunk," "body," "leg." The second element is certainly the Choctaw *lusa,* "black." If the first element is *ąba,* then, the translation is "black hair"; if *ąpi,* then "black leggings," or perhaps "black legs." These Indians had legs, it seems, much darker than their bodies.[114] Being obviously transmitted through the medium of Choctaw, the name cannot mean "salt water"; for the Choctaw would then be either *hąpi oka* or *oka hąpi.*

The Opelousa were a small band, probably a branch of the Atakapa, who once resided in southwestern Louisiana. In 1733 Bienville called a certain Indian tribe the "Loupelousas"; in 1802 des Lozières estimated their number at 130 men; in 1805 Sibley found 40 Appalousas living in a village about fifteen miles west of the Appelousa church. [45] During the second half of the nineteenth century the Opelousa became extinct, or were absorbed by other Indian tribes.[115]

The name of this Indian tribe is perpetuated by that of *Opelousas,* the parish seat of St. Landry. The history of the town dates virtually from 1765, when it became a trading and military post; but it was not officially surveyed until 1805, nor was it incorporated until February 21, 1821. It is at the junction of several important railroads, and in 1925 had a population of 4,437.[116]

OSCA BAY [ˈǫskə]

(a) 1818. *Lake Oscabe.* Ludlow.
   1834. *Oskibe L.* Graham-Tanner.
(b) 1846. *Oskibehat C.* La Tourrette.
(c) 1829 & 1830. *Osca Bay.* T. viii, R. V III. E. Southeastern Dist. of Louisiana.
(d) 1878. *Whiskey Bay.* Gray.
   1895. *Whiskey Bay.* Hardee.

La Tourrette's form *Oskibehat*, though later in date than some others, points clearly to the origin of *Osca*. This name is shortened and corrupted from Choctaw *oski*, "cane," "canebrake," and the intransitive verb *abeha*, "to be in." Evidently, canes were growing in the edge of the water and along the shores of the bay.

The *d*-form probably descends through folk etymology from the alternative Choctaw *uski*, "cane," "canebrake," as the first element. But forms with *uski*- seem not to be recorded. In the vicinity of the bay, which is in the parish of St. Martin, the name *Whiskey* is still commonly heard. Compare the development of *Whiskey Chitto, infra.*

OSCEOLA [o:si'o:1 ə]; [ǫsi'o:1 ə]

The name *Osceola* is a war-title, derived from Creek *Assi-yahola*, "Black Drink Singer." The Creeks brewed a black drink from yupon leaves, and used it during their councils and annual corn festival. Other spellings of the name were *Oseola, Asseola,* and *Asseeholar*. See Hodge, II, 150.

[46] Osceola was the noted Seminole chief who led his people against the United States in the Seminole war of 1835, and who, after baffling or defeating several expeditions sent against him, was treacherously seized under a flag of truce by General Jesup. Osceola died in 1838, at the age of 34, a prisoner in Fort Moultrie, South Carolina.

Osceola has become a popular place name in the United States. In Louisiana the name is borne by a hamlet in the eastern part of Tangipahoa parish, about 14 miles southeast of Amite. Osceola seems to be a comparatively recent settlement: it is not recorded on Hardee's official map of 1895, but is found on maps of somewhat later date—for example, on Cram's map of 1907.

OSHKOSH

Oshkosh is a flag station on the Louisiana and Arkansas railroad, two miles and a half southeast of Chestnut, in the northeastern part of Natchitoches parish. Here, about 1902, Mr. W. L. Golden established a logging camp, which he named after his home in Wisconsin. The camp was abandoned long ago.[117]

Oshkosh was the name of a famous Menominee chief (1795–1858); it is derived from Menominee *ôskôsh*, "claws," a term that is said to have been applied to a member of the social cults of the Sauk, Fox, and Kickapoo tribes. Consult Hodge, II, 160; Hoffman, in *B.A.E., Rep.* 14, Part I,

p. 317 (1896); Legler, in *Trans. Wisconsin Acad. of Sciences, Arts and Letters,* Vol. 14, No. 1 (1903).

OUACHE ['woʃI]

The Ouacha were a small tribe that in 1699 occupied a site probably near the present village of Labadieville, in Assumption parish. In 1718 they moved from their old home and established themselves on the west bank of the Mississippi, not very far above New Orleans. Iberville called the tribe the Ouacha. They were allies of the *Chaouachas,* a name which H. B. Cushman derives from Choctaw *chahachi,* "to ennoble," to raise,"— certainly a very dubious etymology.[118] The meaning of *Ouache,* too, is not clear, because no one has yet ascertained to what dialect the word belongs. Cf. Swanton, in *B.A.E., Bull.* 43, p. 297 ff.; *Bull.* 68, p. 8.

[47] The name of the Ouacha tribe has been given to a lake in St. Charles parish. The following are a few references to the lake:

1732. *Lac des Ouachas.* D'Anville.

1803. *Lac Barataria ou des Ouachas.* Duvallon.

1816. *Quacha Lake.* Darby.

1846. *Lake Washa.* La Tourrette.

1853. *Lake Ouacha or Salvador.* Bayley.

1907. *Lake Ouache or Salvador.* Cram.

Near the southern coast of Terrebonne parish there is a body of water which was long called *Lac Méchant:* see La Tourrette 1846 and Lockett 1882. Popular etmology is responsible for the change of *Méchant* to the present designation of *Merchant.* But Gray's map of 1878 drops *Méchant* in favor of *Washa;* the latter name, indeed, had been used in surveys of 1837–1838, and it is still recorded by some modern maps.

OUACHITA ['woʃItɔ:]

Though numerous guesses have been made as to the origin of *Ouachita,* they have failed to clear up the meaning of the name. "Big Cat river," "Big Cow river," "Big River," "Silver Water," "Male Deer," "Country of Large Buffaloes,"—such are some of the translations of *Ouachita.* In all probability the name is not of Choctaw origin. If it were from the Choctaw, it might be analyzed as a compound of Choctaw *owa,* "hunt" and *chitto,* "big"—that is to say, "Big Hunting Ground." For variant spellings, see Hodge, II, 172; and for comments on the meaning of the name, consult De Bow, XII, 267 (1852); *Early Western Travels,* XVI, 138, fn. 66; *Loui-*

siana Today, Dept. of Agr. & Immigration, p. 178 (1924); *Choctaw Dictionary,* under *owa.*

The Ouachita were a small clan, apparently belonging to the Caddoan family, who resided on the Ouachita river in the northeastern part of Louisiana. At the close of the seventeenth century they numbered five cabins and about seventy men; but their identity seems to have been quite early lost in that of other tribes.

The name of the Ouachita Indians lives in that of a parish and of a river. The original county of Ouachita was established in 1805; it became a parish in 1807, with an area much smaller than that of [48] the old county. The present parish has an area of about 646 square miles; its population in 1924 was 32,168.

Ouachita river, the chief northern tributary of the Red, rises in the western part of Arkansas and enters Louisiana in the northeastern corner of Union parish. It joins Red river approximately thirty miles above the mouth of the latter. That part of Ouachita which is below the mouth of the Tensas, at Trinity, in Catahoula parish, is called Black river.

There is also an old town by the name of Ouachita, on the west bank of the river, in Union parish. Formerly known as Ouachita (Washita) city, it was for many years the center of trade for the surrounding country; but its population is now less than a hundred. It was not incorporated until 1877.

The name *Ouachita* is likewise borne by a station on the Missouri Pacific railroad, in Caldwell parish, as well as by the Ouachita and Northwestern railroad.

It may not be amiss to add that the town of Monroe, Louisiana, occupies the site of the ancient Ouachita Post, which was founded by Don Juan Filhiol in 1785. To this post Filhiol subsequently gave the name of Fort Miro, in honor of Estevan Miró, the Spanish governor of Louisiana (1785–1791). In 1819 the name was changed to Monroe in honor of President James Monroe. During the last quarter of the eighteenth century the post had also acquired the name of *Prairie des Canots* because of its admirable situation as a rendezvous for hunters and trappers. From this point they descended in their canoes to New Orleans, where they found a sale for their furs, bear oil, and buffalo meat. The French of New Orleans called the buffalo meat "viande de chasse."[119]

PANOLA

The Choctaw word for "cotton" is *ponola.* La Tourrette's map of 1846 shows Jane C. Williams to be the owner of "Ponola" plantation, near the present site of Ferriday, in Concordia parish. "Panola" is now the accepted spelling.

[49] PATASSA [pata'sa]

Lockett's map of 1873 records *Patassa* as the name of a bayou in the southwestern part of Grant parish. *Patassa* is a Creole word, derived from Choctaw *nạni patạssa,* "a flat fish," "a perch." Cf. *Patassa, supra.*

PECANIERE; PECAN ISLAND; PECAN POINT

Pecan is derived from the genera name for a nut in various Algonquian dialects, Cree having *pakan,* Ojibway *pagan,* and Abnaki *pagann.* The Indian term embraced all hard-shell nuts, such as the walnut, the hickory, and the hazel nut. In 1786 Thomas Jefferson used the form *paccan-nut.* Besides *pecan* there are other nineteenth-century forms—*pecanne, pecane,* and *pekan.*

The word is usually pronounced pə'ka:n—occasionally [pə'kɔ<:n]—in Louisiana.

Pecaniere is a station on the Gulf Coast lines, nearly six miles south of Port Barre, in St. Landry parish. The local pronunciation is said to be [pakan'jæ:ə]. The name is, of course, formed with the aid of the French suffix -*ière.*

Pecan Island is a post office in the southwestern part of Vermilion parish, about thirty miles southwest of Abbeville. The post office was established about twenty years ago.

The name was first applied to a narrow strip of land, about sixteen miles long, on which grew pecan and live-oak treas. It took its name from the fact that the land was surrounded by sea marsh. The name is recorded on Ludlow's map of 1818.

Pecan Point is the name of a plantation near Grand Bayou, in Red River parish.

PINHOOK BRIDGE

When Lafayette parish was organized in 1823, the parish seat was established at a place called *Pin Hook,* at the site of the present bridge across the Vermilion bayou, about two miles south of the town of Lafayette. It is over this bridge that the old Spanish trail passes. After it had remained at Pin Hook for a short time, the seat of justice was in 1824 removed to Vermilionville, a town which had been founded by Jean Mouten [Mouton] about the year 1821, and had [50] been officially named by the legislature in 1824. In 1884 the name was changed to Lafayette.

There is a tradition that a Frenchman once got into the habit of catching his neighbors' chickens with the aid of a grain of corn on a bent pin, which he tied to a long string and tossed out of his window. Thus his restaurant became famous for its fried chicken, and the site gradually became known as *Pin Hook*.[120]

In the accuracy of this tradition I have little faith. Perhaps *Pin Hook* comes through folk etymology from Choctaw *pinashuk,* "linden," "basswood tree." An ancient Choctaw town called *Pinashshuk* was situated near the present site of Plattsburg, Mississippi. Early references to the linden in Louisiana are not uncommon.[121]

There is also a small farm by the name of *Pin Hook,* about twenty miles west of St. Joseph, in Tensas parish. This farm is situated on a sharp bend in Choctaw bayou, I am informed by the mayor of St. Joseph; and no doubt the form of the bend is responsible for the name of the farm.

PLAQUEMINE ['plækəmen, *infra*]

1732. *Rue des Piakemines.* D'Anville.

1758. *la Rivière des Plaquemines.* Du Pratz, I, 155.

1770. *Bayouc Plakmines.* Pittman.

1802. *Arroyo de Placamine.* Trudeau, Book F, p. 115.

1846. *B. Plaquemine.* La Tourrette.

This name came into Creole French, through the Mobilian dialect, from the Illinois *piakimin, piakimina* (plural), "persimmon."[122] The original variation between *i* and *l* the first syllable appears in Bossu, who says that he dined with the Indians on bears' paws, beavers' tails, and a kind of bread which they called *Pliakmine.*[123] In another paragraph he uses the spelling *piakmine* for a kind of medlar, called *Ougouflé* by the Indians.[124] Charlevoix gives similar testimony as to the popularity of persimmon bread: "Les Sauvages font une pâte de ce fruit, et en forment des pains de l'épaisseur d'un [51] doigt, et de la consistance d'une Poire sèche."[125] Du Pratz, too, comments on this bread. He adds the fact that the Creole French changed the form *Piacminier* to Placminier, "persimmon tree."[126]

There are several pronunciations of *Plaquemine.* ['plækəmən] is extremely common: I also hear ['plækmən], ['plækəmIn], and ['plækmIn]. [Plak'min] is almost entirely confined to spoken French.

Bayou Plaquemine, in Iberville parish, was named long ago because of the large number of persimmon trees that were growing on its banks.

The persimmon tree still flourishes in Louisiana. Two beautiful rows of this tree, according to Mr. Fred Grace, of the State Land Office, formerly extended from the Mississippi river, near Bayou Plaquemine, as far as Mr. Edward Desobry's plantation—a distance of perhaps a mile and a half. Bayou Plaquemine flows out of the Mississippi through the Plaquemine locks towards the west, and then turning sharply towards the south, empties into Grand River; but before making the turn, it is augmented by two streams from the north—Bayou Grosse Tête and Bayou Choctaw. As for Grand River, it reaches the Gulf of Mexico through the Atchafalaya.

The town of Plaquemine is situated on Bayou Plaquemine and the west bank of the Mississippi river, about 14 miles south of Baton Rouge. The town was evidently named after the bayou. Plaquemine was not mentioned by Du Pratz in 1758; but it was recorded by Robin in 1802. It was incorporated in 1838. In 1842 the parish seat of Iberville was removed to Plaquemine from Point Pleasant, which was eight miles farther down the river; and in 1878 the limits of Plaquemine were enlarged and its powers extended by an act of the legislature. The population of Plaquemine is estimated by Mayor Fred J. Wilbert at 6,000.

PLAQUEMINES PARISH

Plaquemines does not differ in its etymology or pronunciation from *Plaquemine,* the name of the town in Iberville parish, *supra.* Plaquemines parish forms the extreme southern end of the state, extending from Orleans parish to the Gulf of Mexico. Plaquemines was organized in 1807, the year when Orleans Territory was divided into nineteen parishes. The first settlement in the parish was made at [52] Point à la Hache, the parish seat, in 1820. The parish contains 100,155 acres, and in 1925 had a population of 12,194.

Plaquemines no doubt took its name either from the old military post of Plaquemine(s), or from that of the bend in the Mississippi river where the fort was built. Here are some early references, a few to the fort and others to the river bend:

(a) 1797. *el Fuerte de Placaminas.* Hill, *Papeles,* p. 103.

1802. *Fort Plaquemine.* Robin.

1803. *Poste de Plaquemine.* Duvallon.

1809. "an old Spanish garrison, called the Plaquemines." Cuming, in *Early Western Travels,* IV, 369.

(b) 1722. *le Detour aux Piakimines.* Charlevoix III, 441.

1732. *Detour des Piaquemines.* D'Anville.

1770. *Detour de Placquemines.* Pittman.

1820. *Plaquemine Bend.* Tanner.

Thirty miles above the mouth of the Mississippi is the bend formerly known as *Plaquemine Bend* or *Turn,*[127] where now stand Fort St. Philip and Fort Jackson. This bend was fortified by the French in 1746, on the recommendation of Lenormant, who at that time was intendant commissary of the French colony. It was here on the east bank of the river, that the Spanish Governor Carondelet built in 1791–2 Fort St. Philip, or el Furete de Placaminas. Evans[128] commented in 1818 on the very elegant appearance of the fort; but Duvallon had criticized most unfavorably its poor equipment and its listless garrison of fifty men.[129] After the cession of Louisiana to the United States, the Fort was occupied by American troops. Its batteries repulsed reenforcements that were coming to the aid of the British after the battle of New Orleans. In 1862 it was damaged by Farragut's guns, but a part of the central building erected by Carondelet is yet intact.

PONCHATOULA [Pǫntʃə'tu:lə]

1808. *Pontchitula.* Pintado, in *Book* Z, p. 39.

1816. *Pontchatoola.* Darby.

1839. *Ponchatoola R.* Tanner.

[53] 1846. *Ponchatwola.* La Tourrette.

1853. *Ponchatoloum Cr.* Bayley.

1814. *Ponchartoula.* Brackenridge.

1871. *Ponchatoula River.* Hardee.

Ponchatoula creek flows through the southwestern part of Tangipahoa parish, and enters the Tickfaw several miles southeast of Springfield, in Livingston parish.

This is a puzzling name. After an examination of the early forms, I reached the conclusion that *Ponchatoula* must signify "falling hair," or "hanging hair," from Choctaw *pāshi*, "hair," and *itula* or *itola*, "to fall," "to hang." This view was strengthened by a letter from Mr. George T. Goodman, of Ponchatoula, Louisiana, who informed me that the Indians gave this fanciful name to the stream because of the abundance of Spanish moss on the trees in its vicinity. He received this information from a half-breed who had been brought up among the Choctaw Indians. It should be recalled here that the early French explorers are responsible for the name "Spanish moss," which they called *Barbe à l'Espagnole,* the Spanish retorting with the nickname *Perruque à la Française.*[130]

Other interpretations of the name are doubtless numerous. I will repeat two which were reported to me by Mr. Goodman. The first is that an Indian girl became ill, and lost all of her hair in one night; hence the place where the tribe had encamped was called "falling hair." Another interpretation is based on the story that Tammany, the noted Delaware chief, wandered to Louisiana and brought with him his son Ochakwa. The latter is said to have been slain by the Indians because of his sympathy for certain captives. When his head was hung by its hair on a tree, the Indians, thinking that the hair sang in the wind, named the place *Ponchitoawa,* "singing hair." Subsequently, the name is alleged to have been corrupted by white settlers to *Ponchatoula.*

Of these two stories the first may be dismissed as fiction, pure and simple; and the second is equally incredible, having in its support not a shred of evidence, either linguistic or historical.

The legend of "Singing Hair" may be due to the translation of *Ponchatalawa* [pɒntʃətæləwə:], the name of the creek in the neighboring parish of St. Tammany. This creek flows almost due west, and [54] empties into the Tchefuncta river, northeast of Madisonville. The Ponchatalawa is recorded on Lockett's map of 1873. The name of the creek is usually translated "singing hair," as if it had sprung from Choctaw *pāshi,* "hair," and *"talowa,"* "to sing." After the story of "singing Hair" had arisen in an effort to interpret the translation of *Ponchatalawa,* the same story might easily have come to be associated with *Ponchatoula,* the name of the creek in the adjoining parish.

But whether *Ponchatalawa* actually means "singing hair," is, I think, very doubtful. It may mean "singing cat-tails," or "singing water flags," the first element in the name possibly being the Choctaw *pancha,* "cat-tail." The creek may have received this name because of the noise made by the wind in the flags along its banks. For a similar reason the Choctaws named Cane bayou *Chelaha,* "noisy," using the term with reference to the sound of the wind in the canebrakes.[131] Certainly, the resemblance between *pancha,* "flag," and the first element of the proper name is so close as to render quite dubious the translation that has hitherto prevailed.

A town, situated three miles south of Hammond, in Tangipahoa parish, took its name from Ponchatoula creek. Ponchatoula is on the main line of the Illinois Central railroad, and has a population of 1,055. It was not incorporated until February 28, 1861.

POOSHEAPATOPE ['pʔʃpətæp]

1813. *Pusthapatapa.* T I, S R 13 E, Greensburg District.
1820. *Pushepatapa Creek.* T I S R 13 E, Greensburg District.
1820. *Pushepetapa Cr.* T 2 S R 14 E, Greensburg District.

1846. *Pooshepatopa C.* La T.
1873. *Poosheepalopa Cr.* Lockett.
1895. *Poosheepalopa Cr.* Hardee.
1925. *Pooshepoatope Cr.* Map Dept. Agr.
1926. *Poosheapatope Cr.* Pub. Ser. Com. Map.

The name of this creek is derived from Choctaw *pushi,* "flour," "meal," plus *patapo,* "pallet," "bed," and it may therefore be freely translated "Sandy Bottom" creek. One may compare the Choctaw adjective *pushi,* "fine, as flour or sand," and such compounds as *tali patapo,* "pavement," *iti patapo,* "bridge," in which the first elements mean respectively "rock" and "wood."

[55] The spellings of 1873 and 1895 are due to a misreading of *t* for *l*; the form of 1846 likewise shows that the "a" of the syllable next to the last was taken to be an "o." This "o" is firmly established on modern maps, though the local pronunciation points unmistakably to the more primitive character of the forms of 1820.

Poosheapatope creek flows through the northeastern part of Washington parish, and empties into Pearl river.

POWHATAN

Powhatan was the name of an Indian village which was situated on an eminence about a mile below the falls of James river, in Virginia. The name was also bestowed by the English colonists of Jamestown on the noted chief and founder of the Powhatan Confederacy, a large group of Indian tribes that occupied the Tidewater region of Virginia. Powhatan died in 1618.

Powhatan is derived from Algonquian *pow'waw* or *po'wah,* "priest," "sorcerer," or "medicine-man," and *-atan,* "Hill," "mountain."[132] Compare the etymology of *powwow. Powhatan* signifies the "hill of the medicine-man." It was on a hill, then, that Powhatan, who was himself the chief sorcerer or medicine-man, conducted his mysterious rites. The derivation of *Powhatan* from Southern Renape *powa'tan,* "falls in a stream," is no longer tenable.

Powhatan is a village on the Texas & Pacific railroad, about eleven and a fourth miles northwest of Natchitoches. In 1902 a station was built on the present site of Powhatan, and was named *Irono.* About three years later the name was changed to *Powhatan.*[133] In 1920 the population was 260.

QUAPAW ['kwɔpɔ:]

Quapaw bayou flows into Cross lake, in Caddo parish. It is given on Hardee's map of 1895. The bayou was named after the Quapaw, a southwestern Siouan tribe, closely related to the Omaha, Ponca, [56] Osage and Kansa. When these tribes separated, those who went down the Mississippi river were called Quapaw, from *Ugaxpa*, "downstream," whereas those who turned up the river became known as *Omaha*, "up stream" people. In De Soto's time the Quapaw were called *Pacaha*, and by de la Vega they were mentioned as the *Capaha*. During the explorations of Marquette and La Salle they acquired the name of Akansea [Arkansas]. In 1829 a band of Quapaw resided on Red river, in the Caddo country of Louisiana. Formerly at least two of their villages were situated on the Mississippi river, and two near the mouth of the Arkansas. In 1925 the Quapaw numbered 1,796 on their reservation in Oklahoma. For variant forms of the tribal name, see Hodge, II, 336.

The view that the name of the bayou is a Caddo Indian form of *papaw* is due to folk etymology.

RICOHOC ['rIko-], ['rIkəhǫk]

Ricohoc is the name of a plantation about ten miles below Franklin, in the parish of St. Mary. The station of Ricohoc is on the Southern Pacific railroad, five miles northwest of Patterson. I have not been able to find out exactly when the station was named, either from the postmaster at Patterson, or from Mr. H. S. Palfrey, of Franklin, Louisiana, whose father formerly owned the plantation. But Ricohoc is given by Cram in 1905.

Ricohoc I suspect to be of the same origin as the Indian place names *Rickahake* and *Rickahock* of Virginia colonial history. Formerly identified with the Cherokee, the Rickohockan are now thought to have been probably the Erie, a powerful Iroquoian tribe, who were also known as the Erigà, Rique, Rike-haka, etc.[134] The name *Rickohockan* may be an aphetic form of the Onandaga *tsho-eragk*, "raccoon." By the French the name was translated "chat sauvage." The Rickohockans were an Iroquoian tribe who lived on the southeast shore of Lake Erie, and who were also called the Erie, Eriga, Erighek, and Erich-ronnon. To the French they were known as the "nation du chat"; but the fact, though familiar to every student of history, must be repeated that the French term for "raccoon" was "chat sauvage." The Rickohockans, driven from their home by some hostile Iroquois, are said to have reached Virginia about 1655. The [57] view, however, that certain early place names in Virginia are identical in origin with Erie, "raccoon," becomes disputable when one learns that Indian towns by the name of *Richkahauck* and *Rickahake* existed in Virginia before the alleged advent of the Erie or Rickohockans. John White's map of 1586 also shows a town by the name *Ricahokene* in North Carolina. Subsequently, it is true, mention is made of the place "Rickahock" (1689). The suspicion is strong that these names are all corrupted from the Algonquian *rekau,* "sand" and *"haki,"* "place."[135] It is possible, indeed, that they may be derived from the Virginia Indian *arocoune, aroughcun,* "raccoon," and *"haki,"* "place." Consult Hanna, *The Wilderness Trail,* 1, 8, 9, 15, 33 (1911); and for a different translation of *Erie,* see Hodge, I, 430.

ROANOKE

Roanoke is the name that the Virginia Indians gave to small disk-shaped beads, made of shells and used as money and as ornaments. These beads were mentioned by Smith in 1612 under the name of *rawrenock,* and again in 1624 under that of *rawranoke.* The name is derived from Southern Renape *rârenawok,* the plural of *rârenaw,* which in turn is a derivative of the stem *râr,* "to be smoothed, polished," and *naw,* "body."[136] In the Ashmolean Museum, of Oxford, England, there is, or was, a specimen of "Virginia purses imbroidered with Roanoake" [1656].[137] Some other early spellings are *Roenoak, Ronoak, Roanoack, Roenoke.*

The town of Roanoke, Louisiana, is situated on the Southern Pacific railroad, five miles and a half west of Jennings, in Jefferson Davis parish. Until approximately 1895 the site of Roanoke was known as Esterley; at that time the name was changed to Roanoke by G. W. and J. M. Booze, two brothers who had formerly lived on a plantation near Springwood, Virginia. The population is about three hundred. The local pronunciation is said to be 'ro:əno:k.

SANTA BARB

Santa Barb, a creek or bayou in Natchitoches parish, undoubtedly owes its name to Choctaw *Sinti bok,* "snake creek." On page 76 of [58] the *American State Papers,* Vol. IV (1825), ed. Green, the name appears in three different spellings—*Santa Barbara, Centerburg,* and *Santaburg.*

Santa Bogue, the name of a creek in Washington county, Alabama, points even more clearly to the same origin.

SHONGALOO ['ʃɔ:ŋ:əlu:]

The source of *Shongaloo* is the Choctaw *Shākolo,* "cypress tree." In the northern part of Webster parish there are two towns named *Shongaloo*—the one *Old,* the other *New Shongaloo.* Both are shown on Lockett's map of 1873. The old town is near Cypress bayou, about a mile and a half from the Arkansas line. Its population, according to Professor E. D. Perkins, is about one hundred. Fifty years ago it was an important meeting ground for the citizens of Louisiana and Arkansas, I am informed by Professor E. S. Richardson.

The new town is situated on Indian bayou, a few miles south of the old town. New Shongaloo has a population of about 300.

ST. TAMMANY

Tammany is derived from Delaware *Tamanend*, "the affable," the name of the noted Delaware chief of the seventeenth century. Other forms of the name are *Tamanee, Tamanen, Tamany, Tamened, Taminy,* and *Temane.* During the Revolutionary War his admirers adopted him as their patron saint, and celebrated his festival on the first of May. His name was conferred on St. Tammany parish, in Louisiana, because of the large number of Indians who formerly resided there. No white men settled in this parish before the middle of the eighteenth century. In 1811 the parish was established, and in 1829 Covington was chosen as the parish seat; but ten years prior to the latter date the northern part of the parish had been named *Washington,* and in 1869 a large part of St. Tammany became known as Tangipahoa parish. St. Tammany contains 590,720 acres; its population in 1924 was 21,357.

TALISHEEK ['tælIʃi:k]

Talisheek is clearly from Choctaw *tạlushik*, "gravel," "pebbles." The name is found on Lockett's map of 1873. Talisheek is a small [59] station in St. Tammany parish, on the New Orleans Great Northern railroad, about 22 miles south of Bogalusa. St. Tammany, like the parishes of Washington and Tangipahoa, has deposits of sand and gravel.

TALLA BENA ['tælə'bi:nə]

Talla Bena, a plantation in Madison parish, is on the Missouri Pacific railroad, about five miles north of Tallulah, the parish seat. The plantation was established about 1840 by Mr. Thomas P. Roe. Its population is now about 100.

The first element of the name *Talla Bena* is Choctaw *tala*, "palmetto"; the second is Choctaw *bina* or *abina*, "camp." The name was first given to a bayou which runs through the plantation, and was then transferred to the plantation. The interpretation of *Talla Bena* as "Big Bayou," which is that current among the people of the neighborhood, is quite misleading. In this vicinity there were several Indian settlements. The Choctaws covered their huts with palmetto leaves, building the frames of small saplings and making the huts either round or rectangular. For a picture of a Choctaw hut, see Bushnell, *Bulletin 69, B.A.E.*, p. 65 (1919).

TALLULAH [tə'lu:1 ə]

Tallulah is derived from Cherokee *talulu*, but the meaning of the name has been lost. Talulu was an ancient Cherokee settlement, situated at some distance above the famous falls in Georgia.[138]

If *Tallulah* were of Choctaw origin, its meaning would be clear. The Choctaw *talula* is a Sixtowns form that signifies "bell"—literally, "sounding metal," from *tạli*, "metal," and *ola* or *ula*, "to sound," "to ring."

After the organization of Madison parish in 1839, Richmond was chosen as the seat of justice. During the Civil War this town was practically destroyed, and the parish seat was transferred to Delta. In 1883 the seat was removed to Tallulah. Tallulah is situated at the intersection of the Missouri Pacific and the Vicksburg, Shreveport and Pacific railroads. Its population is about 3,000.

Shortly after the Civil War a telegraph operator named Tallulah station in honor of his sweetheart, whose home was at Tallulah Falls, [60] Georgia. The name is spelled *Tallula* on Hardee's map of 1871, but the modern form is given on Lockett's map of 1873.

TANGIPAHOA ['tænd3Ipə'ho:]

(a) 1699. *Tandgepao* (river). Pénicaut, in Margry V, 387.
            Tangipahoes (tribe). Iberville, in French, 1, 24 (1869).
    1718. *Tangipaos* (tribe). de l'Isle.
    1732. *Tanzipao R.* d'Anville.
    1846. *Tangipahoa R.* La Tourrette.
(b) 1682. *Tangibao* [village] Membré, in Shea, *Discovery*, 174.
    1684. *Tanzibao.* Franquelin, in Thomassy, *Géol. Prat.*, facing p. 16.
    1699. *Tangibao* (tribe) Iberville, in Margry IV, 120.
(c) 1804. *Tanchipaho Rio.* Pintado, in *Lib.* D No. 4 G. p. 124.

The origin of the name *Tangipahoa* has been the subject of considerable comment. Pénicaut says that in the Indian tongue it means "white corn." This is incorrect: the Choctaw for "white corn" is *tâsh haksi*. A second attempt to analyze the word is that of Du Pratz, who assigns to the little river *Tandgi-pao* the meaning "bled grôle"—"parched corn." The origin of *grôlé* is obscure. Professor Grandgent, to whom I referred the word, cites Du Cange's *grollare*, "movere," Fr. *grouiller*, and certain East French forms:

Savoyard *Grolá,* East French *gruler, greuler.* Meyer-Lübke, as Professor Grandgent further observes, connects the East French forms with Mid. High Ger. *Griuwel.* The meaning of the verb must early have been confused with that of *griller.* I note that Godefroy has *groller,* in the sense of *rissoler, griller. Gröler* signifies, then, "to shake," "to parch." My colleague Professor H. A. Major says that the Creoles still use the verb in such phrases as *farine grôlée,* "parched flour," *maïs grôlé,* "parched corn." The parched flour is used instead of talcum powder. The corn is first shelled and then parched; when ground and cooked with water or milk, the corn forms an ingredient in a dish that Professor Major calls *'go:fio.* Is this related to French *gaufre,* "waffle"? I must not forget to add that Du Pratz, describing the manner in which the Indians parch corn, uses the phrase "grôler ou roussir."[139] Joutel prefers the form *grouler.*[140]

[61] But whatever the ultimate source of *grôlé* may be, Du Pratz's translation of *Tangipahoa* is erroneous, the Indian name containing no element that may be rendered by this participle. A third attempt to translate the name is that of Gatschet, with whom Halbert, a noted student of the Choctaw dialect, was in accord. Gatschet derives the name from Choctaw *tanchapi,* "cornstalk," "cob," and *ayua (aioa),* "gather"—"cornstalk gatherers."

Only one more interpretation of the name deserves to be mentioned— namely, Bushnell's. Bushnell derives *Tangipahoa* from Choctaw *tonche,* "corn," and *pahoha,* "cob" or "inside," asserting that the Choctaw themselves translated it "corncob."[141] Whether this translation is preferable to Gatschet's is difficult to decide, especially because the Choctaw dictionary fails to record the word *pahoha.* Then, too, one may seriously doubt whether the Choctaws of this day have retained a knowledge of the exact origin of the word.

The Tangipahoa Indians lived near another tribe called the Acolapissa, in the region east of New Orleans, and particularly on the Tangipahoa river. Whether the Tangipahoa tribe formed a seventh village of the Acolapissa, and like the Acolapissa, spoke Choctaw, has not been ascertained. The village of the Tangipahoas is said to have been destroyed by the Oumas.[142]

The name of the Tangipahoa tribe survives in that of a river, a town, and a parish. The river, rising in Mississippi, runs nearly south about seventy miles, and falls into Lake Pontchartrain, some distance southwest of Madisonville. The town was incorporated on March 13, 1866, and in 1920 had a population of 252. It is on the Illinois Central railroad, about ten miles north of Amite. The parish of Tangipahoa was established in 1869 during the administration of Henry Clay Warmoth. It has become famous as the strawberry centre of the south. It contains 505,600 acres, and in 1924 had a population of 32,377.

TCHEFUNCTA [tʃI'fʌŋktə]

1732. *Kefuncté R.* Danville.
1758. *Quefoncté R.* Dupratz, map, I, facing p. 138.
1776. *Chefoncto R.* Romans.
[62] 1816. *Chifuncté.* Darby.
1895. *Tchefunta River.* Hardee.

Tchefuncta is taken from Choctaw *hachofakti,* a "chinquapin." Du Pratz writes of the name as follows: "On arrive à la Rivière de Quéfoncté, ou des Chạtaignes-Glands; elle est longue et belle, et vient des Chatkas."[143]

Some maps, such as Nicholson's of 1880 and Lockett's of 1882, show a place spelled *Tchefuncta,* about ten miles northwest of Covington. This place has apparently disappeared, but the spelling *Tchefuncta* is now used for the name of the river, though the Geographic Board recommends *Chefuncte.*

The Tchefuncta river flows southward through western St. Tammany, and joins the Bogue Falaya south of Covington; from there the united streams flow through Madisonville into Lake Pontchartrain.

TCHOUPITOULAS [tʃọpI'tu:ləs], *infra*

1718. *Choupitoulas.* Pénicaut, in French, 1, 141 (1869).
1719. *Tchoupitoulas.* Cruzat: see *La. His. Quar.,* 1, 3, 121.
1719. *Chapitoulas.* Cruzat: see *La. His. Quar.,* 1, 3, 234.
1721. *Le village des Chapitoulas.* Census of Nov. 24.
1722. *Chapitoulas.* Pénicaut, in Margry, V, 578.
1722. *Les Chapitoulas.* Charlevoix, III, 438.
1732. *Les Chapitoulas.* d'Anville.
1765. *Chapitoulas.* Ross.
1770. *Chapitoula.* Pittman, *Mississippi Settlements,* 58. (Hodder ed.)
1796. *Chapitoulas.* Hill, *Papeles,* 17, 150.
1803. *Barrio de Chapitulas.* Trudeau, *Lib.* D. No. 4 G, p. 23.
1803. *Côte des Chapitoulas.* Duvallon, *Vue,* 49.
1812. *Quartier des Chapitoulas. ASP,* II, 346. G. & S.
1823. *Chapitoulas. ASP,* III, 511. G.

Though the two earliest forms of this name have "ou" in the first syllable, they are undoubtedly less primitive than those that have "a." The evidence is indeed overwhelming that the latter offer the sole clue to the mystery of this peculiar name,[144] which was originally [63] applied to an important French settlement above New Orleans, on the east bank of the Mississippi beginning at the bend in the river where Southport now stands. It was here that the Chauvin brothers, famous in the history of Louisiana, established their plantations. The name is thought to have been derived from that of a small Indian tribe, possibly akin to the Choctaws, whose village was situated at the bend in the river; but the records do not justify any conclusion as to the exact origin of the tribe. The name is perpetuated by that of a street in New Orleans and by a plantation, the latter occupying the site of the old Indian village.

The etymology of *Chapitoulas* or *Tchoupitoulas* is obscure, because nobody knows to what dialect the name belongs. If it is of Choctaw origin, then it may perhaps be analyzed as a compound of *hacha*, "river," *pit*, "at," and *itula*, *itola*, or *itonla*, "reside,"—literally, "those who live at the river." Cf. Choctaw *hina yat olanli pit itonla*, "to live near the road." The loss of the initial syllable of the Choctaw *hacha* is like that in *Chappepeela, supra;* the meaning of the name reminds us of the translation of *Bayou Goula*— "Bayou people."

If the analysis of *Chapitoulas* is uncertain, the source of the form *Tchoupitoulas* is perfectly clear. As early as May 24, 1723, reference is made to a "Bayou Chaptoulas,"[145] which had its head waters on the Chapitoulas settlement. Recalling now the fact that one of Pénicaut's names for Bayou St. John is *Choupic*,[146] we at once become aware of the origin of the spelling *Tchoupitoulas:* it results from a blend of *Choupic* and *Chapitoulas*, the latter designating not merely the settlement that lay "three leagues" above New Orleans, but also the bayou that rose on the settlement and ran down as far as the city. That yet another bayou—the one which Du Pratz calls *Tchoupic*[147]—contributed to the evolution of the form *Tchoupitulas* is far from improbable; for the name of this bayou was doubless familiar in the vicinity of New Orleans long before it appeared in Du Pratz's book.[148] Trudeau's plan of New Orleans, drawn in 1798, shows a Bayou Tchoupitoulas; nor have all traces of this bayou been obliterated in Jefferson parish.[149]

[64] To follow minor variations in the spelling of the New Orleans street would serve no useful purpose. I have observed, however, the following:

1823. *Tchoupitoulas. ASP,* III, 519. G.

1834. *Tchoucpictoulas.* Graham-Tanner.

1846. *Tchopitoulas.* La Tourrette.

1878. *Choupitoulas.* Gray.

Of more interest than these changes in form is the pronunciation of the name. This is almost always ʼtʃopIˈtuːləs; occasionally, however, the final *s* is silent. In a quarter of New Orleans that bears the nickname of "Irish Channel," *'tʃæpI'tu:ləs* prevails—a pronunciation generally considered incorrect.

TENSAS ['tɛnsɔ:]

In 1682 a small Indian tribe by the name of the Taënsa inhabited the shores of Lake St. Joseph, in the present parish of Tensas. It was here that Iberville in 1699 found seven Taënsa villages. By 1715 the Taënsa had moved to the vicinity of what is now the town of Edgard, in the parish of St. John; by 1764, to the mouth of Bayou Lafourche. Between these two dates they had resided elsewhere; and they made other changes of habitat until they became extinct or were absorbed by neighboring tribes. The origin of their name is unknown. Gatschet's suggestion that it comes from Choctaw *tanchi*, "corn," is untenable. Consult Swanton, *Bulletin* 43, *B.A.E.*, (1911).

Tensas parish and Tensas river perpetuate the name of this tribe. The parish was created in 1842 from the northern part of Concordia. It has an area of 632 square miles; its population in 1920 was 12,085. Tensas river rises in southeastern Arkansas, and flows southward through the parishes of East Carroll, Madison, and Tensas. In East Carroll and a part of Madison it is called a bayou. It joins the Ouachita and Little rivers in Catahoula parish, at Trinity, an old town which takes its name from its site at the confluence of the three streams.

TICKFAW ['tIkfɔ:]

(a) 1804. *Rio Go Tickfoha.* Trudeau's Survey, in *Book* D, No. 4 G. p. 106.
[65] 1806. *Riv. Ticfoha.* Lafon.
(b) 1816. *Tickfah R.* Darby.
(c) 1805. *Rio de S Vicente ô Tickfaw.* Pintado's Survey, in *Lib.* J. p. 12.
   1806. *Tickfaw Creek. ASP,* I, 822.
   1846. *Tickfaw R.* La T.

In the first example under (a) the word *go* is apparently due to the carelessness on the part of the surveyor, who seems to have transferred it from the initial syllable of another proper name on his plat.

Of the three styles of spelling that are recorded above, the first is nearest to the Indian source of *Tickfaw;* for the second element of the name is obviously the Choctaw *foha*, "rest," "ease." The first element I take to be a contraction of the Choctaw *tiak*, "pine." If this analysis is correct, the word signifies "Pine Rest." The loss of the "a" in *tiak* resembles that of the second syllable in the usual American pronunciation of *diamond;* indeed, the Choctaw itself elides vowels in a similar manner, as for example in *Ok-tibbeha*, which is contracted from *okti*, "ice" and *abeha*, "to be in."

The Tickfaw river, rising in the state of Mississippi, flows through a beautiful region of pines in the parishes of St. Helena and Livingston, and falls into Lake Maurepas about six miles northeast of the mouth of the Amite.

The town of Tickfaw is situated on the Illinois Central railroad, eight miles north of Hammond, in Tangipahoa parish. The population of Tickfaw in 1920 was 318. The town is recorded on Lockett's map of 1873.

TIOGA [tai'o::ə]

Tioga is derived from Iroquois *teyogen*, "anything between two others," or from *teihohogen*, "at the forks of rivers."[150] Earlier forms are *Diahoga*, *Teahoge*, *Teugega*. The Tioga river of northern Pennsylvania and Steuben county, New York, unites near Corning, New York, with the Conhocton to form the Chemung. The name *Tioga* has also been given to counties in Pennsylvania and New York, as well as to towns in other states than Louisiana.

Situated at the junction of the Missouri Pacific and several other railroads, the village of Tioga is about five miles north of Alexandria, [66] in Rapides parish. In 1920 its population was 585. Tioga was founded by the Louis Warner Lumber Company, and in 1900 was named by Mr. Frank Clark. The site of the town was formerly called Levine.[151]

TUNICA ['tju:nIkə]

Gatschet connects *Tunica* with Chickasaw *tunnig*, "post," "pillar," thinking of a post as a boundary mark of the Tunica territory on Yazoo river;[152] but Halbert says that the word means "the people," and that it springs from Tunica *ta*, "the," *uni*, "people," and the noun suffix *-ka*.[153] The latter is the correct analysis. For variant spellings, see Hodge, II, 839; and for the kinship of Tunica with Chitimacha and Atakạpa languages, consult Swanton, in *Bulletin* 68, *B.A.E.* (1919).

Tunica is a name that belongs respectively to a group of hills, a bayou, and a village in West Feliciana parish. The bayou was called Willing's Bayou[154] as late as 1799; but in 1816 Darby gave it as *B. Tonica*, and in 1818 Ludlow used the modern spelling. Rising in the Tunica hills and flowing southward, the bayou empties into the Mississippi, about a mile south of Tunica.

The village is situated on the line of the Louisiana Railway & Navigation Company, in the northwestern part of the parish. Formerly it was a boat landing on the east bank of the Mississippi; and though now farther away from the river, it is still virtually reached by the Mississippi during the season of high water. In 1820 the hamlet was called Tunica Village; in 1853, Tunica P.O.; in 1871, Tunica; between 1880 and 1899, often Bayou Tunica. Finally, in 1906 the name was changed to *Wilhelm,* in honor of the Kaiser; but on May 27, 1918, *Tunica* was restored.[155] The population in 1920 was only 86.

The name *Tunica* perpetuates that of an Indian tribe, living at the close of the seventeenth century on the southern side of the Yazoo river, not very far from its mouth. It was among the Tunica Indians [67] that Father Davion labored for approximately twenty years; his final departure from them took place in 1719 or 1720. In 1758 the Tunica occupied a village seven leagues above the fort at Pointe Coupée; in 1803 fifty or sixty "Tounicas" were still residing in the same neighborhood.[156] From this settlement they subsequently moved to a site on the lower Red river, near the present village of Marksville; and here about twenty-five survivors, of whom almost all are of mixed blood, are still to be found.

WASHLEY

1846. *Washley Cr.* La Tourrette.

If Washley is of English origin, it may spring from an OE *wæsc,* "small stream," plus *lēah,* Mercian dative *lēge,* "clearing"—the "clearing by the small stream."[157] Subsequently *Washley* may have come to be used as a personal name.

Washley, however, may not be English; it may have come from Choctaw *wushulli* or *wosholli,* a substantive formed in turn from the verb that signifies "to ferment," "to form a froth on the surface." A free translation would be "Foam Creek." I recall here that the Indians are said to have named Lake Bistineau "Big Broth" because of the foam on its surface when the water was high. In its form *Washley* reminds one of the development of *Bushley, supra.*

Washley creek empties into the Tangipahoa river, in the upper southern part of Tangipahoa parish. A postoffice by the name of *Washley,* situated not far from the eastern boundary of Tangipahoa, is of comparatively recent origin.

WAUKSHA ['wɔ:kʃə]

Oct. 12, 1807. *Bayou Wauxshie.* William Darby's Field Notes, T 5 S R. 4 E.

1816. *B. Wauksha.* Darby.

Wauksha is not from the Choctaw; it is the Potawatomi *Wauktsha*, which signifies "fox." The bayou was probably named by an early trader or trapper who was familiar with words from various Indian [68] dialects.[158] Bayou Wauksha empites into Bayou Courtableau, in St. Landry parish.

WAXIA

Waxia is the name of a hamlet on Bayou Wauksha, in St. Landry parish; *v. Bayou Wauksha, supra.* Thirty-nine years ago Mr. R. Lee Hawkins applied for a post office on Bayou Wauksha. Upon granting his request, the post office department asked him to select a shorter name. The result was *Waxia*, which Mr. Hawkins writes me is pronounced like Wauksha.

WEYANOKE ['waiəno:k]

Weyanoke is traced by Gerard to the Lenape *winak*, "strong-scented wood," "sassafras"; but this explanation is rejected by Tooker, who connects the name with Algonquian *waen-ohke* or *ween-ohke*, a compound of *waenu*, "going around" and *ohke*, "land"—that is to say, "river bend."[159] The principal village of the Weanoc Indians, who belonged to the Powhatan confederacy, was indeed situated in 1608 on land within the bend of the James river, about twenty-miles above Jamestown. In 1617 the plantation of Weyanoke was established, and in 1631 a Mr. John Flood was mentioned as the burgess from Westover, Flowerdieu Hundred, and Weyanoke.[160] Captain John Smith's name for the tribe was *Weanocks*.[161] During the first half of the eighteenth century the name of the Virginia plantation was written in various ways—*Waynoak, Weynoak, Wynoack, Wayanoak, Wyanoke, Wyonoke*, etc.[162]

The Louisiana plantation by the name of *Weyanoke* is on the west bank of Big Bayou Sara, about four miles west of Wakefield, in the parish of West Feliciana.[163] Mr. Robert S. Towles, of Bains, Louisiana, informs me that his father, Mr. John Turnbull Towles, who was a native of West Feliciana, married Miss Frances Peyton [69] Eskridge, of Virginia; and that it was she who in all probability selected *Weyanoke* as the name of their plantation in West Feliciana.

WHISKEY CHITTO CREEK ['hwIskI'tʃItə]

1846. *B. Whiskey Chitto.* La T.
1895. "   "   "   Hardee.
1926. *Whiskey Chitto Cr.* Map, Pub. Ser. Com.

The unanimity of the forms reveals the source of *Whiskey Chitto* as Choctaw *uski* or *oski*, "cane," "canebrake" and Chit(t)o, "large"—in other words, "Big Cane creek." A similar corruption of Choctaw *uski* or *oski* is evident in the local pronunciation of Osca bay, *supra,* and also in the evolution of *Wiskey* creek, a name which Ludlow's map of 1818 assigns to the northeastern part of Hancock county, Mississippi.

Whiskey Chitto creek crosses the northeastern boundary of Beauregard parish, and empties into Six Mile creek, in the parish of Allen.

WINONA

Winona is derived from Dakota *Winona,* which signifies "first-born—if a daughter." In Longfellow's *Hiawatha* the name appears as *Wenonah.* If the first-born was a boy, the Dakota name was *Chaskay.*[164]

Winona, a station on the Chicago, Rock Island & Pacific railroad, is about 8 miles north of Winnfield, in the parish of Winn. Approximately a quarter of a century ago the site was named *Winona* by the Pine Tree Lumber Company, which was owned by people from Winona, Minnesota. The timber has all been cut, and nothing is left of the station but the name on a board near the railroad.[165]

WOODCHUCK

Popular etymology has corrupted Cree *wuchak* into *woodchuck.*

Woodchuck is the name of a station on the Texas & Pacific railroad, 1¾ miles south of Gayle, in Caddo parish.

[70] WYANDOTTE

The origin and signification of the name *Wyandotte* are obscure. Hale thinks that it means "people of one speech";[166] Hodge, that it probably means "the islanders," or "dwellers on a peninsula."[167] Some early forms are *Guyandottes, Ouendats, Owendots, Vendats, Wondats,* etc.[168] The Wyandots were a member of an Iroquoian group of tribes, by the French called Hurons, who inhabited a part of Canada southeast of Lake Huron on the Georgian bay. In 1883 the name of the tribe was given to an American breed of fowls.

Wyandotte is the name of a plantation, on the Southern Pacific railroad, near Addis, in St. Mary parish. The plantation was called thus in 1899, because the owner liked the sound of the name.[169]

YUPON ['juːpǫn], occ. ['joː]-, rarely ['jɔː]-

Yupon is derived from Catawba *yopun,* a diminutive of *yop,* "tree," "shrub." This beautiful evergreen is found throughout Louisiana; its leaves were brewed by the southern Indians in the making of a famous black drink. See Hodge, I, 150.

Yupon is a station not far from Erwinville, on the New Orleans, Texas & Mexico line, in the parish of West Baton Rouge.

[71] ADDENDUM

Pawnee is a hamlet on the Missouri Pacific Railway, in Allen parish.

The name is thought to be derived from Pawnee *pa'riki*, "horn," a term designating the resemblance between a Pawnee's scalp-lock and a powder-horn. The Pawnee tribe belongs to the Caddoan family.

INDEX OF PLACE-NAMES

NOTES

1. Margry, V, 385.

2. *EWT,* V, 238, 239.

3. Cf. Gatschet, I, 113, Chamberlain in the *Nation,* vol. 59, p. 381 (Nov. 22, 1894).

4. *B.A.E.,* Bull. 48, p. 6 (1909).

5. Gatschet, I, 125.

6. *A Half Century of Conflict,* I, 343. Centenary ed.

7. See Swanton, in *B.A.E.,* Bull. 73, Plate 7 (1922).

8. *Noms Géographiques de la Province de Québec,* etc., pp. 17–18 (1906). I have not seen the second edition of this study.

9. See Margry, IV, 178.

10. See Thomassy, *Carte* following p. 226.

11. See Halbert, in *Trans. Alabama His. Soc.,* III, 65–66 (1898–99).

12. See *Géol. Prat.,* p. 220.

13. *The History and Geography of the Mississippi Valley,*5 I, 245 (1832).

14. *Louisiana As It Is,* p. 104 (1876).

15. Margry, IV, 178.

16. French, I, 116 (1869).

17. Margry, VI, 249.

18. See Swanton, in *B.A.E.,* Bull. 43, p. 24 ff. (1911).

19. *ASP,* III, 526. G. (1834).

20. *ASP,* III, 210. G. (1834).

21. Branner, in *MLN,* xiv, 35–36 (1899).

22. Walker, pp. 218–219.

23. See *De Bow,* XII, 267 (1852).

24. *Histoire,* II, 240.

25. See *De Bow,* XII, 267 (1852).

26. *Voy.,* III, 8 (1807).

27. *ASP,* III, 77 (1816). G.

28. *EWT,* XVII, 69.

29. *Louisiana,* p. 173 ff. (1817).

30. Cf. von Engeln and Urquhart's *The Story Key to Geographic Names,* p. 96 (1924).

31. Deiler, *The Settlement of the German Coast of Louisiana,* etc., p. 60 (1909).

32. *Lib.* VII, H, facing p. 71.

33. *Voyage à la Louisiane,* p. 241 (1802).

34. *Lib.* D N 4 G, p. 48.

35. See R. R. Hill, *Papeles Procedentes de Cuba,* 142, 128, 133 (1916).

36. *An Account of Louisiana,* pp. 6, 7 (1803).

37. See *Second Voyage à la Louisiane,* J, 85 (1803).

38. Cf. Joutel, in Margry, III, 353, 379.

39. For an interesting description of Caddo lake, see the New Orleans *Times-Picayune,* Sept. 5, 1926.

40. See *ASP,* III, 83. G & S.

41. Margry, IV, 373–374.

42. Margry, IV, 442.

43. *De Bow,* III, 228 (1847).

44. *De Bow,* XII, 257, 267 (1852).

45. See Hodge, I, 212–213.

46. See Margry, IV, 192, 193, 194, 195, 425.

47. Cf. Gatschet, I, III.

48. *Voy.,* 241, fn.

49. *Ibid.,* 241, fn.

50. *Voy.*, II, 309 (1807).

51. *ASP,* I, 732, *Indian Affairs* (1806).

52. See Perrin, *Southwest Louisiana,* pp. 13, 14 (1891).

53. Halbert, in *Miss. Reg.*, 446 (1917); cf. *Choctaw, infra.*

54. *Mississippi Official & Stat. Reg., Cent. Vol.*, p. 446 (1917).

55. Cf. Du Pratz's description of this fish, in *Histoire*, II, 158.

56. Margry, V, 385.

57. French, I, 146 (1869).

58. *Histoire*, I, 45–46.

59. *Ibid.*, I, 46, fn.

60. *His. Coll.*, I, 47 (1869).

61. Margry, V, 387.

62. For example, Du Pratz, II, 219; Bossu-Forster, *Travels*. . . . , I, 34 (1771).

63. *History of Natchitoches,* 16 (1920).

64. *ASP,* III, 141. G. (1834).

65. *De Bow*, XI, 44 (1851).

66. Cf. Gatschet, I, pp. 108, 137.

67. *Emigrant's Guide,* p. 44 (1818). On Darby's map the tribal name is *Quachatta.*

68. *EWT,* xvii, 69.

69. *ASP,* Ind. Affairs, I, 728.

70. Cf. Branner, *MLN,* XIV, 37 (1899).

71. Joutel, in Margry, III, 409.

72. Cf. Hodge, under *Anadarko,* I, 51–52.

73. *B.A.E.*, Rep. 14, Pt. 2, 1893, p. 1103.

74. *Voy.*, III, 15.

75. *Louisiana Studies,* pp. 183, 184 (1894).

76. *History of Natchitoches,* p. 10 (1920).

77. Survey T. 14 N.R. 12 W. NW Dist. La. 1832.

78. Beauchamp, pp. 106–107.

79. Cf. Margry, IV, 176.

80. See Swanton, in *Bull.* 43, p. 29 (1911).

81. *EWT,* XIII, 312.

82. Cf. the New Orleans *Times-Picayune* for Sunday, April 11, 1926, Section 4, page 1 ff.

83. See Pénicaut, in Margry, V, 395.

84. On the origin of *Baton Rouge,* see Scroggs, in *Proc. His. Soc. of East & West Baton Rouge*, Vol. I, 20 ff. (1906–07); and Butler, *ibid.*, p. 39 ff.

85. Cf. Gatschet, I, 108, 137.

86. See Deiler, *German Coast,* pp. 106–107.

87. Cf. Margry, IV, 172.

88. Cf. Margry, IV, 187.

89. *ASP,* III, 97. G. & S.

90. *ASP,* III, 111. G. & S.

91. *ASP,* III, 132. D. G.

92. *ASP,* III, 210. D. G.

93. *ASP,* III, 98. G &. S.

94. See Robertson, *Louisiana Under the Rule of Spain*, etc., II, 208; *ibid.*, II, 143 (1911).

95. *Géol. Prat.*, 222.

96. *Histoire*, I, 141.

97. Cf. a paper of mine in *Englische Studien*, XLVII, ii, 8 (1914).

98. A convenient *résumé* of these names is given by T. L. Thompson, in *Pub. La. His. Soc.*, IX, 92 ff. (1917).

99. See Iberville, in Margry, IV, 118, 121, 157, etc. (1699).

100. *His. Col.*, I, 22, 26, etc. (1869).

101. See, respectively, French, II, 224 (1850); Du Pratz's *Hist.*, I, 141; Dumont's *Mem. His. sur la Louisiane. . . .* , I, 3 (1753).

102. See, for instance, Margry, IV, 251, 260.

103. *A Concise Natural History of East and West Florida*, 304 (1775).

104. *Views of Louisiana*, 282, 284 (1814).

105. See *B.A.E.*, Bull. 43, p. 48 (1911).

106. *ASP*, III, 202, G.

107. See Margry, IV, 178.

108. Cf. Gatschet, I, 43; Hodge, II, 1 ff.; II, 35.

109. See Margry, V, 494–537, VI, 197, 200; 215–216; 224–225; *De Bow*, VI, 107 ff. (1848).

110. For further details, see French I, 107 ff. (1869); Parkman, *A Half Century of Conflict*, I, 355, Centenary edition; Fortier, *Louisiana*, II, 410–412.

111. See Hodge, under *Nadowa*, II, 87.

112. Courtesy of Mr. L. C. Randolph, of Bayou Goula, La.

113. See *B.A.E.*, Bull. 43, p. 302 (1911); Du Pratz, II, 241.

114. See W. J. Sandoz, in *La. Hist. Quar.*, Vol. 8, No. 2, p. 225 (1925).

115. See Swanton, in *B.A.E.*, Bull. 43, pp. 363–4 (1911).

116. For an interesting sketch of Opelousas and St. Landry parish, see W. J. Sandoz, in *La. Hist. Quar.*, Vol. 8, No. 2, p. 221 ff. (1925).

117. Information kindly furnished by Mr. U. P. Breazeale, of Natchitoches, La.

118. *A History of the Choctaw, Chickasaw and Natchez Indians*, p. 497 (1899).

119. For an interesting account of the early settlement of the Ouachita region, see H. Bry, in *De Bow*, III, 225 ff. (1847).

120. See Griffin, *The Attakapas Trail*, p. 12 (1923).

121. See Darby, *Emigrant's Guide*, pp. 34, 99, 100 (1818).

122. Cf. "piaquiminia," Margry, III, 444 (1687).

123. Forster's Translation, Vol. I, 189 (1771).

124. *Ibid.*, Vol. I, 347.

125. *Journal*, III, 395–6 (1721).

126. *Histoire*, II, 18 (1758).

127. Gayarré, *Louisiana*, II, 34 (1852), calls it *Plaquemine Turn*.

128. *EWT*, VIII, 350.

129. *Vue de la Colonie Espagnol. . . .* , p. 67 (1803).

130. Pénicaut, in Margry, V, 389.

131. Cf. Bushnell, in *B.A.E.*, Bull. 48, p. 7 (1909).

132. See Tooker, in the *Amer. Anthropologist*, N.S. 6, p. 467 (1904).

133. For this information I am indebted to Mr. Frank J. Burke, Land & Industrial Commissioner of the Texas & Pacific Railway.

134. Mooney, quoted by Bushnell, *B.A.E.*, Bull. 69, p. 37 (1919).

135. Cf. Ruttenber, *Indian Geog. Names*, 87 (1906).

136. See Gerard, in the *Amer. Anth.*, N.S., IX, 106 (1907).

137. See Bushnell, in the *Amer. Anth.*, N.S., IX, 38–39 (1907).

138. See Mooney, in *B.A.E.*, Rep. 19, Part I, 417 (1898).

139. *Histoire,* II, 5; cf. I, 153–4.

140. Margry, III, 343; cf. 376, 400, 408.

141. See *B.A.E.* Bull. 48, 2 (1909).

142. Margry, IV. 168; cf. Swanton, in *Bull.* 43, 284 (1911).

143. *Histoire,* I, 154.

144. Cf. H. P. Dart, in *La Hist. Quar.*, VII, 2, 308 (1924).

145. See Cruzat, in *La His Quar.*, I, i, 109.

146. See French, I, 146 (1869).

147. *Hist.,* I, 45–46 (1758).

148. On the nature of linguistic blends, see Jespersen, *Language,* 312 ff. (1924).

149. See M. S. Soniat's interesting paper on "The Tchoupitoulas Plantation," in *La. His. Quar.*, VII, 2, 309 (1924).

150. See Beauchamp, pp. 94, 231, 261.

151. Courtesy of Miss Maude M. Clark, of Tioga, La.

152. *Mig. Leg.*, I, 41.

153. *Pub. Miss. His Soc.*, V, 305 (1902).

154. *De Bow,* III, 122, fn. 7 (1847).

155. Mr. J. N. Campbell, of Shreveport, Louisiana, has kindly given me the dates of the last two changes.

156. *An Account of Louisiana*, p. 24 (1803).

157. Cf. Mawer and Stenton, *The Place-Names of Bed. and Hunt.*, p. 201 fn. (1926).

158. Cf. Kellogg, in *Wis. His. Soc. Proc.*, p. 231 (1909).

159. *Amer. Anthr.*, N.S. 6, 681 (1904).

160. *Journals of the House of Burgesses of Virginia*, p. X (1619, 1658–59), 1915.

161. Arber's *Smith*, I, 51 (1910).

162. *Burgesses*, p. 440 (1712–26); Arber's *Smith*, II, 984.

163. Information kindly furnished by Mr. E. M. Percy, of Baton Rouge, the present owner of the plantation.

164. See Dunn, *True Indian Stories,* pp. 317–318.

165. Information kindly furnished by Miss Estelle Tannehill, of Winnfield, La.

166. Cf. Dunn, *True Indian Stories,* 319 (1909).

167. Hodge, II, 584.

168. Hanna, *The Wilderness Trail,* II, 457.

169. Courtesy of Mr. Percy O'Brien, of Rhoda P. O., Louisiana.

2

More Indian Place Names in Louisiana

BY WILLIAM A. READ

Professor of English, Louisiana State University

Louisiana Historical Quarterly, XI, July 1928

PREFATORY NOTE

My former study of the Indian place names of Louisiana[1] contains a few errors, which I wish to correct in the present paper. I am, too, now able to give a few facts about various names; and, what is more important, I can add other names that are still extant, as well as some that seem but recently to have fallen into disuse. I also include several names which, though ultimately from Indian sources, have become an integral part of the English vocabulary. Perhaps it may be well to say that I have not as a rule discussed those names which have long been obsolete, nor have I made any remarks, except in one or two cases, on street names of Indian origin.

In searching the surveys of the State for place names, I have been materially aided by Miss Mary Graham and Mr. Carl Campbell, both of the State Land Office. My best thanks are likewise due to Mr. James A. McMillen, librarian of the Louisiana State University, and to Mr. Robert J. Usher, director of the Howard Memorial Library, for help on the bibliography of my subject; to my colleague, Professor H. A. Major, for information with regard to certain Creole-French terms; to Mr. G. H. McKnight of Colfax, for data on the geography of Natchitoches parish; to Mr. A. T.

Witbeck, of Shreveport, for numerous communications on the geology and early history of Northwest Louisiana; and to Dr. John R. Swanton, of the Bureau of American Ethnology, for valuable comments on the etymology of sundry place names.

ADDENDA ET CORRIGENDA

The following references are to the pages of my previous study:

P. 3. Dr. Swanton kindly points out to me that the Atayos, who were mentioned by De Vaca in 1529, cannot be identical with the Adai; that De Vaca evidently had in mind the Tonkawan band called *Toho*.[2]

[446] P. 16. An alternative name for Lake Cannisnia, in De Soto parish, is recorded on Lafon's map of 1806 as *Pisaquie*. This name, which seems never to have become very popular, is of Algonquian origin and signifies "buffalo"; compare the Ojibway *pizhiki*, "buffalo," and the Menominee *pisaxkiu*, "cattle."[3] The "x" in the Menominee form has the value of "ch" in German *ach*. A slightly different derivative of the Indian word appears in the English translation of Marquette and Joliet's narrative of [447] 1673: "We call the *Pisikious* wild buffaloes, because they very much resemble our domestic oxen; they are not so long, but twice as large."[4]

P. 23. For "Gariennie," read "Gaiennie."

Pp. 28–29. On the difficult name *Dorcheat* interesting information has been given me by Mr. S. L. Herold as well as by Mr. A. T. Witbeck. The account of the Freeman-Custis exploration of Red River in 1806 contains, it seems, the following statement with respect to Bayou Datché, now known as *Dorcheat:*

> On the morning of the 11th they reached a place where a branch of the river or bayou ran rapidly in from the north. Being informed by Mr. Touline, a French gentleman born in the Caddo nation and who accompanied the party of that nation to render his good offices, that it was absolutely impracticable to pass the great raft in boats of any kind; as neither red nor white men had attempted it for fifty years before, and that this was the only communication through which the passage could be effected; they here left the river and entered the

4. Du Pratz's map of Louisiana

bayou. This bayou is by the Indians called Datché (which in their language signifies a gap eaten by a bear in the log), from the circumstance of the first Indian who passed this way seeing a bear gnawing a log in this place.

Touline's interpretation of the old form of *Dorcheat* would be trustworthy if it were sustained by the vocabulary of the Caddo dialect. Unfortunately, no Caddo word expresses anything in the remotest degree resembling the sense of the phrase "gap eaten in a log by a bear"; nor, yet more unfortunately, is the syntax of the Caddo tongue concise enough to render in two syllables the equivalent of the English translation. The Caddo for the "bear eats a hole in the log" would run somewhat like this: "Dughamako yako saha na-oustse dahughnouehsa"—literally, "hole log in bear he eats." Touline's analysis seems to bear the misleading earmark of Indian tradition: indeed, the Indians themselves may utterly have forgotten the real source of the name.

P. 34. The name *Kisatchie* is found as *Cossachie* in *Sibley's Report from Natchitoches in 1807*, pp. 30, 31, 32, 47.[5] The form *Cossachie* confirms my derivation of the name from Choctaw words that signify "Reed river."

[448] P. 36. The identity of *Manchac* with the Mobilian *imashaka*, "rear entrance," is rendered more plausible by my discovery of the form *Mashake*, the name of a stream, on the "Draught of the R. Ibbeville" that accompanies Pittman's *European Settlements* (1770). The first "a" in *imashaka* is nasalized.

P. 42. I see now that Gatschet connects the Caddo *Nataché* with the Choctaw *Natassé*, "to press," "to squeeze."[6] This etymology impresses me as being highly improbable; in all likelihood the two words have nothing whatever to do with each other.

P. 55. For "steam," read "stream."

P. 58. For "admires," read "admirers."

P. 59. That *Talla Bena* signifies "Palmetto camp" is verified by the words *Bina chito*, the Choctaw for "Big Camp," which Carlos Trudeau wrote on a survey of the vicinity of Bayou Talla Bena. The survey is dated January 14, 1804.[7]

Pp. 59–60. My statement as to the time when Tallulah, in Madison parish, received its name needs correction. Shortly before the outbreak of the Civil War the chief engineer of the old Vicksburg, Shreveport & Texas railway named a station on this road *Tallulah* after his boyhood home in Georgia. The charter for the railroad was granted on March 20, 1856. Mr. Linton W. Stubbs, who was a division engineer on the Vicksburg, Shreveport & Pacific railroad more than forty years ago, gave this bit of information to Mr. A. T. Witbeck; and Mr. Witbeck kindly transmitted it to the author of this paper. A slightly different version of the naming of Tallulah is related by Mr. W. M. Murphy, in "The History of Madison Parish" *(La. Hist. Quar.*, January, 1928, p. 42).

P. 67. It is not necessary to derive *Wauksha* from the Potawatomi *waukt-sha*, "fox." A more plausible source is the Choctaw *wakcha*, "forked." Of the two main branches of Bayou Wauksha, in St. Landry parish, one bears the name *Little Wauksha*.

P. 69. My colleague, Professor B. H. Singletary, reminds me that the phrase "Six Mile creek" should be changed to "Calcasieu river."

[449] LIST OF ADDITIONAL NAMES

ACASA

In 1805 Sibley makes mention of Lac Occassa, which was situated in the southern part of the Natchitoches parish.[8] Some other forms of the name are the following:
Lake Acassa: Survey T 7 N–R 6 W, La. Mer., 1809.
L. Cassi: Darby's map of 1816.
L. Cassim: Tanner's map of 1820.
Lake Acasa: Survey T 7 N–R 7 W, La. Mer., 1848.
The bed of the lake has long been dry. The pronunciation and the meaning of the name seem to have been forgotten. Nevertheless Sibley's form *Occassa* may be regarded as a syncopated derivative of Choctaw *oka hushi*, "waterfowl," or, perhaps more reasonably, of Choctaw *okak asha*, "swans are

there,"—that is to say "Swan lake." The wild swan was formerly common in Louisiana. But I am not sure that the name is of Indian origin. Possibly the source is the French *Lac d'Acacia*, "Locust-tree lake."

AMITE

Several modern writers affirm that the name *Amite* commemorated the friendly reception which the French settlers on the Amite river received at the hands of the Indians. The word *Amite* certainly looks like a corruption of *amitié;* and towards the end of the eighteenth century *amitié* no doubt came to be considered the source of the name by some of the inhabitants of Louisiana. I have not succeeded, however, in finding any support of this view in the writings of the early French explorers. Iberville, Joutel, Péni-caut, Dumont, La Harpe, Charlevoix—none of these even mention the river, if one may except the occurrence of the name on the Bellin map in Charlevoix's work; nor does Du Pratz, fond as he was of commenting on the etymology of place names, throw any light on the source of *Amite*. He described the stream merely as "la Riviere d'*Amité*, qui est assez grosse, & qui a un cours de soixante-dix lieues dans un fort beau Pays."[9] The name is given as "Mité R." on the Bancroft copy of Delisle's map of 1718, as the "Amit" by D'Anville (1732–1752), as "R. Amitte" by De Crenay (1733), and as the [450] "Amite R." by Bellin (1744). In 1765 Ross records the "Amit River or Lamique," a phrase in which the latter form, whether it be dialectal French for *L'Amitié* or simply an error on Ross's part, appears too late to merit serious consideration.

Inasmuch, then, as neither the early explorers nor the early cartographers apparently connect the name of the river with *amitié*, I have reached the conclusion that the modern writer who seeks in *amitié* the source of the relatively late form *Amite* is deceived by a verbal resemblance between the two words; that the name of the river is not derived from French *amitié*, "friendship," but was in all probability corrupted by the French explorers from the Choctaw adjective *himmita*, "young,"—a term not strikingly novel in view of the curious designations that Indians have bestowed on watercourses. When *himmita* had once become corrupted to *Mité*, the further shift to *Amité* naturally took place through a misunderstanding of the word-group *La Mité*, the vowel of the definite article being taken as the first letter of the proper name. From *Amité* to *Amitié* was then but another false step. In a somewhat similar fashion *Calcasieu*, "Crying Eagle," has erroneously been identified with French *quelque chose or quelques choux; Mal-bancha*, "the Mississippi river," with French *male bouche;* and the first element of *Chappepeela,* "Hurricane river," with French *chapeau.* The first "a" in the Choctaw *Malbancha,* I should observe, has approximately the sound of the vowel in *gull.*

The view that *Mité* arose from *himmita* becomes all the more reasonable when one considers the large number of aphetic forms that have descended from Indian names. Thus a glance through my former study reveals the fact that the Indian sources are each longer by an initial syllable than are the words *Cahoula, Chafalia, Catahoula, Chacahoula, Chappepeela, Chicka-maw, Chickima, Chinchuba, Colapissa, Mentou,* and *Tchefuncta.* In contrast with these distorted forms, the earliest French names are so well preserved that one is rarely in doubt as to their origin. *Chandeleur, Dauphine, Maure-pas, Pontchartrain,* and a host of other names attest the early explorers' familiarity with the French tongue. An educated Frenchman like Delisle would never have sanctioned such a form as *Mité* if he had known a current French word to be its source. Evidently, neither Delisle nor any other French cartographer was aware of the origin of the name *Amite.*

[451] Finally, it is significant that none of the local pronunciations of *Amite* ever retain the final vowel sound of the French *amitié.* There seem to be two pronunciations, almost equally common. In the first pronunciation, for which my authority is Mr. Harry D. Wilson, commissioner of Agriculture and Immigration, the "A" has the value of the vowel in *ham;* the "i," that of the vowel in *meet.* In the second the "A" has the value of the vowel in *tame;* the "i," that of the vowel in *mitt.* In both pronunciations the stress seems to me to waver between the first and the second syllable, according to the well-known law of rhythm.

The Amite river, rising in the southwestern part of Mississippi, drains several Louisiana parishes and empties into Lake Maurepas. At Head of Island the river forms a small fork called *Petite Amite,* which I have often heard pronounced as if it were the English word-group *Pit Amit.*

The town of Amite is situated on the Illinois Central railroad, sixty-eight miles north of New Orleans. Mr. Harry D. Wilson kindly informs me that the town was named *Amite City* about 1852, but that subsequently it dropped the second part of the name. The population is estimated at 2,500.[10]

ARIZONA

Arizona, a hamlet situated in the central part of Claiborne parish, was incorporated on March 1, 1869.

Egli regards the name *Arizona* as a Spanish adaptation of the Pima

Indian *a-ri,* "small," and *son,* "spring."[11] Hodge, however, derived it from *Arizonac,* probably "small springs" or "few springs," the name of a former Papago rancheria, in Sonora, Mexico, just below the present southern boundary of Arizona.[12] The name has nothing to do with Spanish *arida zona,* "arid zone."

Mr. J. M. Oakes, postmaster at Arizona, writes to me that he does not know who selected the name for the hamlet.

ATHAO

The Little, or Athao, river is a small, deep stream in the southeastern part of Natchitoches parish.[13] *Athao* is evidently intended for *Natao,* the name of one of the eight Caddo tribes [452] that Iberville observed on his trip up the Red river in March, 1699.[14] The Natao are technically known as the *Adai,* a term which is derived from the Caddo *hadai,* "brushwood."[15]

Mr. G. H. McKnight, who is thoroughly familiar with the country about Little river, informs me that he cannot remember ever having heard any one use the Indian name of the stream. The local pronunciation of *Athao* seems to have been forgotten. But *Athao* is still recorded on the map of Louisiana issued in 1916 by the Department of the Interior.

BILOXI

Biloxi bayou connects Lake Eugenie with Lake Borgne, in the parish of St. Bernard.[16]

Biloxi is a Mobilian corruption of *Taneks āya* or *Taneks āyadi,* the name by which the Biloxi Indians called themselves. The whole name signifies "First People."[17] In Louisiana, the "o" of *Biloxi* is generally pronounced like the "u" of *luck.*

"As early as the year 1699, the French, under Iberville, built a fort on the east side of the Back Bay of Biloxi, and called it Fort Maurepas, the site of which is now the town of Ocean Springs. A little later, in 1701, under orders from home, the colony was removed to Mobile Bay, the capital of French Louisiana, was again located at Old Biloxi in 1718, and in 1721 the colony was removed to the present city of Biloxi and from there [1722] to New Orleans."[18]

CHETIMACHES

The designations that once kept alive the memory of the Chitimacha tribe seem almost all to have passed away. *La Fourche des Chétimachas,* for example, has been simplified to *La Fourche,* and *Lake Chetimaches* of Darby's map (1816) has become the *Grand Lake* that waters the parishes of Iberia, St. Mary, and St. Martin.

The tribal name, however, survives as that of a street in Donaldsonville, where, according to Mrs. Charles E. Coates, of Baton Rouge, it is written *Chetimaches* and is pronounced as if it were spelled *Chetty-matches.* In this pronunciation the initial [453] "ch" sounds like that in *chin;* the last two syllables are exactly like the English word *matches.* The stress is on the syllable next to the last.

Gatschet says that the name *Chitimacha* is of Choctaw origin, and that it signifies "they have" (imāsha) "cooking vessels" (*shuti*).[19] On the history of the tribe, consult Swanton,[20] and for variant forms of the name, see Hodge.[21]

CHIHUAHUAITA

Chihuahuaita was the name of a station on the Woodworth and Louisiana Central railway in Rapides parish; but the tracks have been removed, and consequently the station no longer exists. Mr. James C. Bolton, of Alexandria, La., who had kindly furnished this information, is not aware of the reason why the name was selected. That it must at any rate have been suggested by *Chihuahua,* the name of a Mexican city and state, requires no proof.

In reply to my request for aid on the etymology of *Chihuahua,* Señor Luis Castillo Ledón, director of the Museo Nacional, Mexico City, promptly wrote that the word signifies "place of manufacture"; that it is composed of the Nahuatlan *Chihua,* "que equivale à *hacer,* y *hua* que significa que *tiene.*" The word ends of course in the diminutive suffix *-ita,* as in Spanish *bonita.*

Chihuahuaita takes the chief stress on the high tense "i" of the syllable next to the last, and a secondary stress on the first "hua." One may acquire the pronunciation of the name by adding a stressed *-ita* to the usual American pronunciation of *Chihuahua.*

CHINQUAPIN

Chinquapin is the name of a gully in Allen parish.[22]

Gerard derives *chinquapin* from the Virginia Renape *chinkomen* or *chinkwemen,* "rattle-nut," the component elements of the word being *chinkwan,* "a rattle," and *-men* or *-min,* "nut." The suffix, however, has been replaced by *-pin,* "a root."[23]

[454] COLEWA

Bayou Colewa, in the parish of West Carroll, is shown on *Survey* T 20 N–R 9 E, La. Mer., 1852. In the same year the name of the bayou is given as *Coelwa,* on Silas Taylor's survey marked T 22 N–R 10 E. A branch of the bayou by the name of *Little Colewa* is sketched as early as 1838, on *Survey* T 19 N–R 9 E, La. Mer. Finally, the name is corrupted into *Coularra* by some recent maps of Louisiana.

The evidence that I have obtained with regard to the history of this name is conflicting. Mr. W. F. Derrick, postmaster at Pioneer, La., thinks that the name is a corruption of *Coldwater.* On the other hand, Mr. S. H. Campbell, postmaster at Oak Grove, La., asserts that the name was first used by a band of Choctaws, who had rested on the bank of the stream while they were on their way from Mississippi to the West. One of these Indians, known to the settlers as Indian Joe, is said to have remained on the bayou for several years. This information was given to Mr. Campbell by Mr. James B. Drake, a Confederate veteran of eighty-three years, who has lived in Oak Grove all his life.

Assuming the word to be of Choctaw origin, I am, nevertheless, at a loss as to its exact signification. Perhaps it is derived from Choctaw *kalowa,* "notched," "jagged," which may possibly have been used in the special sense of "crooked." This is the most plausible interpretation that I can suggest. A definitive solution, however, is quite difficult by reason of the fact that the first part of the name points to Choctaw words as widely divergent in meaning as *oka,* "water," *okla,* "people," *coi,* "panther," and *kali,* "a spring of water." The "a" in *kali,* one should observe, has nearly the sound of "u" in *sun.* The second part of the name, if the derivation from *kalowa* seem far-fetched, may be connected, though doubtfully, with Choctaw *laua,* "many, much, abundant."

Mr. C. H. Neely, of Oak Grove, assures me that the name is pronounced *Colewah.* In this form *Cole* sounds like *coal,* and *wah* like the first two letters of *wad.* The stress is on the first syllable.

[455] FAQUETAIQUE

Faquetaïque is the name of a polling precinct and a prairie in St. Landry parish, I am informed by Judge Gilbert L. Dupre, of Opelousas. The name is pronounced like a French word of the form *Facquitaïque,* with the stress on the final syllable. A few variant forms are:

Prairie Faketike: Ludlow's map of 1818.

Prairie Faquetyke: Lockett's map of 1882.

Prairie Faquataique: Hardee's map of 1895.

Faquetaïque is derived from Choctaw *fakit tek,* "turkey-hen." Prairie Faquetaïque must evidently have been a favorite haunt of the wild turkey. This game bird is still found in some parts of the State.

HICKORY

The popularity of the name *Hickory* is attested by its appearance in three different places on modern maps of Louisiana. The state has a Hickory Valley in Winn parish, another hamlet called *Hickory* in Avoyelles, and a Hickory branch, a stream that crosses the southern boundary of Beauregard parish and joins the west fork of Calcasieu river.

Hickory Valley was so designated in 1874 because of the heavy growth of hickory trees in its vicinity. A post office, but no town, is there. For these facts I am indebted to Mr. S. R. Newsom. The hamlet of Hickory in Avoyelles parish had a population of but 50 in 1920. Hickory branch, which Lockett in 1873 called "Hickory Cr.," received its present name on a survey of 1879, earlier surveys seeming to indicate merely the course of the stream.

The word *hickory* is derived from the Virginia Renape *pakahikare,* "it is brayed," a term applied to an emulsion which the Indian women prepared from the nuts of several species of hickory, and used to flavor soups and boiled vegetables. The name *hickory* was transferred by white settlers from the emulsion to the tree.[24]

[456] MANGROVE

Mangrove bayou is an affluent of Calcasieu lake in Cameron parish.

The first element of *Mangrove* is adopted from Spanish *mangle,* "mangrove," which is derived in turn from the Arawakan language of Haiti. The second element is due to confusion with English *grove.*[25]

MONGOULOIS

Lake Mongoulois, situated in the parish of St. Martin, was named in memory of the Mugulasha, an Indian tribe that lived with the Bayogoula above Bayou Lafourche, on the west bank of the Mississippi. *Mongoulois* is evidently a French coinage of the same kind as *Danois, Hongrois,* and *Iroquois,* in which the suffix *-ois* serves the purpose of indicating a race name. I have observed no variant spellings, a survey made in the winter of 1832–33 giving, like Hardee in 1895 and the War Department's map of 1925, only the form *Mongoulois*. The French pronunciation of *Mongoulois* is generally so much altered that the first syllable rhymes with *song* and the last syllable loses its "w"; the middle syllable sounds like French *goût*. The stress is shifted to the first syllable.

The tribal name *Mugulasha* is composed of the Mobilian *im*, "their," *ougoula*, "people," and *asha*, "are there." It signifies "people of the opposite clan."[26] In 1699 Iberville writes the name *Mougoulachas*;[27] La Harpe gives it as *Mongoulacha*.[28]

OPOSSUM

Opossum creek is a tributary of the Comite river, in the parish of East Feliciana. The name of the creek is shown on the War Department's map of Southern Louisiana (1915), revised to 1925.

Opossum is adapted from the Virginia Renape *apasum*, "white" beast, an aphetic and dialectal form of *wapasum*.[29] The Choctaw name for the opossum is similar in meaning: *shukata*, literally "white hog," from *shukha*, "hog," and *hata*, "white." [457] The first "a" in *shukata*, as well as that in *hata*, has the sound of "u" in *hut*. For variant forms of *opossum*, one should consult the *New English Dictionary*.

The early French explorers of Louisiana refer to the opossum as "rat de bois." Thus in 1687 Joutel gives a description of certain animals, which he compares to rats, though he does not use the exact term "rat de bois." Nevertheless he clearly has in mind the opossum.[30] Subsequently, in 1721, Charlevoix applies the name "Rat de Bois" to an animal that can be no other than the opossum;[31] and in 1807 Robin says: "Je rencontrai un opossum, que dans le pays on nomme rat de bois."[32]

My colleague, Professor H. A. Major, whose mother tongue is French, is perfectly familiar with the term "rat de bois"; but he cannot remember ever to have heard the word *opossum* in the French dialects of Louisiana. Littré cites *opossum* and the variant "rat des bois"; for the latter there seems to be no authority in Louisiana French of the present day.

PASCAGOULA

Two bayous by the name of *Pascagoula* are found in Louisiana, the one in Caddo and the other in Red River parish. Mr. J. Fair Hardin, of Shreveport, points out to me that the former is included in the rough sketch of Red river made by Captain Henry M. Shreve in 1833. This bayou is shown on *Survey* T 15 N–R 12 W, La. Mer., 1833 and 1834.[33]

The latter bayou, as I learn from Mr. A. T. Witbeck, was recorded by John Dinsmore in 1814, on *Survey* T 12 N–R 9 W, La. Mer.

The Pascagoula Indians formerly resided on the Pascagoula river, in the southern part of Mississippi, where they were encountered by Iberville as early as 1699. An admirable summary of the subsequent wanderings and fate of this small tribe is given by Hodge;[34] interesting details of its history are furnished by Swanton.[35]

[458] The legend of the mysterious music said to be heard on the Pascagoula river forms the subject of a newspaper article by Frank A. Lewis.[36]

Pascagoula is derived from the Mobilian *paska ougoula*, "bread people," a term that is the equivalent of the Choctaw *paska okla*. In *paska* the first "a" sounds like "u" in *hut*. One of the Pascagoula chiefs went by the significant name of "Big Bread."[37]

POCOSIN

On Clinch Grey's survey of 1821 Pocosin creek is shown as a tributary of the Tangipahoa river in the southeastern part of Tangipahoa parish. On the War Department's map of Southern Louisiana, revised to 1925, the name is spelled *Pocasin*. In Vernon parish there is also a Pocosin creek, which empties into Bayou Anacoco.

Gerard derives *pocosin* from the Virginia Renape *pakwesan*, "a swamp," "a place covered with shallow water," *pakwesan* being a compound of the stem *pakw-*, "to be somewhat dry," and *-sen*, "put" in the condition expressed by the stem.[38] Tooker gives a different interpretation, which is quoted by the *New English Dictionary*, under *pocosin*.[39] As the name of a river in Virginia, the word is said to occur as early as 1635 (*NED*).

QUEBEC

Quebec is a hamlet in Madison parish, about six miles by rail west of Tallulah. As the name of a plantation, *Quebec* is found before the Civil War, I am informed by Mr. W. M. Murphy, of Tallulah. The name of the city from which that of the hamlet is taken is written *Kébec* by French authors of the first half of the seventeenth century. *Québec* is generally thought to be of Algonquian origin: compare, for instance, Micmac *kebek*, "strait," "narrows." The name was applied to the Canadian city because of its site at the place where the St. Lawrence river becomes narrow.

Mr. Pascal Poirier has recently suggested what I take to be a less convincing etymology. He thinks that the Indians may [459] have borrowed the word from the French explorers; that the second syllable is French *bec,* "beak," "promontory," and that the first syllable may perhaps have lost a final "l." See "Recherches sur l'Origine du Mot de Québec," in *Mémoires de la Société Royale du Canada,* Vol. XX, Sec. III, Sec. I, Mai 1926, pp. 93–98.

RACCOON

Raccoon Pass is the name of a strip of water that separates Little Bird island from the southeastern shore of Plaquemines parish. There is also a Raccoon pass off the southern shore of Lafourche parish.

Raccoon is a derivative of the Virginia Renape *arakun,* an abbreviated form of *arakunem,* "He scratches with the hands" the bark of the trees.[40] Captain John Smith says (1607–1609): "There is a beast they call *Aroughcun,* much like a badger, but useth to liue on trees as squirrels doe."[41]

It is now interesting to learn that the French of Louisiana have abandoned the term by which their forefathers designated the raccoon. That this term was long ago considered inapt becomes clear from a remark made by Du Pratz. "Le chat sauvage," he says, "a été mal à propos ainsi nommé par les premiers François, qui ont été à la Louisiane; car il ne tient du Chat que la souplesse, & ressemble plutôt à la Marmote."[42] Instead of "chat sauvage" the Creoles of Louisiana use the word *chaoui,* I am told by my colleague, Professor H. A. Major. *Chaoui* is unmistakably a loan from the Choctaw or Mobilian *shaui,* "raccoon." The incorrect spelling *chatoui,* recorded by Fortier, is doubtless the result of a typographical error.[43]

SODO

Sodo or *Soda* is the name that was applied to a large lake near the present site of Shreveport. This body of water was formed not earlier perhaps than 1770 or 1780, I am informed by Mr. A. T. Witbeck. It has been drained by a large canal.

[460] Fortier notes that the name *Caddo lake* has often been given to a chain of lakes extending above Shreveport and consisting of Clear, Cross, Ferry, Sodo, Swan, and Roberta.[44] What is usually known as *Sodo* or *Soda lake* appears in 1827 as *Sheodo* on Burch and Lee's map of Red river. Captain Henry M. Shreve spells the name in ways varied enough to arouse suspicion that he had no idea whence it is derived. Beginning with *Soder* in 1833, he uses *Soda* in 1835 and follows the latter with *Sota* in 1839.[45] La Tourrette's map of 1846 has the form *Sodo,* whereas some later maps prefer the spelling *Soda.*

The first authoritative statement as to the source of this name is made by Sibley, who writes in 1805 that the Caddoques "live about thirty-five miles west of the main branch of Red river, on a bayou or creek, called by them Sodo, which is navigable for perogues only within about six miles of their village, and that only in the rainy season. They are distant from Natchitoches about one hundred and twenty miles, the nearest route by land, and in nearly a northwest direction. They have lived where they do now only five years."[46]

This assertion of Sibley's effectually disproves the view that *Sodo* may be a corruption of the proper name *De Soto* or of some French phrase like *chute d'eau,* "waterfall." *Sodo* is of Caddo origin. Possibly it may be connected with Caddo *shoehdaugh,* "hunter, warrior"; compare Burch and Lee's form *Sheodo.*

TIGOUYOU

Martin gives *Tigouyou* as the name of a bayou that enters Lake Pontchartrain on the side of the city of New Orleans, higher up than Bayou St. John.[47] Darby's map of 1816 and Tanner's of 1839 show a Bayou Tiguyou on the lake shore in what is now St. Charles parish, whereas the Graham-Tanner map of 1834 places Tigouyou correctly in Jefferson parish, farther to the east and much nearer to Bayou St. John. Though the name is still familiar to some of the older residents of New Orleans, the stream is now called *Indian bayou,* I have learned from Captain Joseph P. Loga, of New Orleans. The Captain pronounces the name [461] like a compound of English *tiger* and *you,* with the stress on the first syllable.

It is now interesting to observe that there was on the shore of Lake Pontchartrain an ancient portage to which La Harpe, in his account of Iberville's departure from the Bayogoula and Mougoulacha, assigns the name *Tigonillou.* La Harpe's words are: "Le 10 [October, 1699] il partit de ces villages. A quatre lieues au-dessous il arriva au portage de Tigonillou, qui rend au lac, et qu'on a depuis nommé la ravine de Sueur."[48] Le Sueur was a Canadian soldier and explorer. The name *Sueur R.* on Ross's sketch of 1765 shows that the portage must have been in the vicinity of the present site of Frenier, in the parish of St. John.

If we will turn again to the passage from La Harpe, we shall be struck at once by the resemblance between La Harpe's *Tigonillou* and Martin's *Tigouyou;* for the "ll" of the former name undoubtedly has the value of "y," and the "n" may well be a misprint for "u." *The resemblance between the two forms is actually so close as to arouse the conjecture that the Indians used the name *Tigouyou* for more than one bayou on the shore of Lake Pontchartrain.

The origin of *Tigouyou* is unknown. Dr. Swanton suggests to me that it may perhaps be composed of Choctaw *tiak,* "pine," and *ahoyo,* "where a search was made." I should not hesitate to derive the first element of the work from Choctaw *iti,* "forest," and the second from Mobilian *ougoula,* "people," if I could find other instances in which a French *y*-sound has replaced the Mobilian "l."

TUSCUMBIA BEND

Tuscumbia Bend was the name of a curve in the old main bed of the Mississippi River, on the eastern boundary of Madison parish. This name, though recorded in *The Century Atlas of the World* (1899) and on some recent maps of Louisiana, is no longer used, I am assured by Mr. W. J. Hossley, mayor of Vicksburg. *Tuscumbia* is, however, the name of a river in Mississippi and of a town in Miller county, Missouri. The same name, too, is borne by the capital of Colbert county, Alabama. Tuscumbia was a [462] Chickasaw chief who resided near the present site of the Alabama town; its name perpetuates his memory.

Tuscumbia is clearly a popular corruption of the Choctaw or Mobilian war-title *tashka abi,* "Warrior Killer." Such a title was usually conferred on a warrior as a token of his valor in battle. The etymology of the name becomes all the more plausible when one remembers that the first "a" in tashka, "warrior," and the "a" in abi, "killer," have approximately the sound of the vowel in *sun.*[49]

NOTES

1. Louisiana State University Bul., February, 1927.

2. Cf. Hodge, *Handb. Amer. Ind.,* II, 771 (1906).

3. *Archaeol. Amer.,* II, 340 (1836); *Bur. Amer. Ethn.,* Rep. 14, Part I, 310 (1893).

4. French, *Hist. Coll.,* 285 (1850).

5. Museum of the American Indian, 1922.

6. *Trans. of the St. Louis Acad. of Sci.,* V, 54 (1888).

7. See *Book D, No. 4 G,* p. 108.

8. Annals of Congress, 9th Cong., 2d. sess., col. 1093. Washington, 1852.

9. *Histoire,* I, 153 (1758).

10. Cf. Fortier, *Louisiana,* I, 38 (1914); Mrs. Percy McCay, in the New Orleans *Times-Picayune,* January 23, 1927.

11. *Nomina Geographica,* p. 53 (1893).

12. For further details, see Hodge, *Handbook,* I, 87.

13. See *Survey* T 7 N–R 6 W, La. Mer., 1809.

14. Margry, *Mémoires*, IV, 178.

15. Powell, in *B.A.E.*, Rep. 7, p. 45 (1891).

16. "Biloxi" is the spelling on *Survey* T 12 S–R 17 E, St. Helena Mer., 1846.

17. Swanton, in *B.A.E.*, Bul. 47, p. 5 (1912).

18. Dunbar Rowland, *History of Mississippi*, II, 746 (1912).

19. *A Migration Legend of the Creek Indians*, I, 44 (1884).

20. *B.A.E.*, Bul. 43, pp. 337–360 (1911).

21. *Handbook*, I, 286 (1906).

22. See *Survey* T 4 S–R 4 W. La. Mer., 1886.

23. *Amer. Anthrop.*, N.S., IX, 89.

24. See Tooker, *Amer. Anthrop.*, N. S. VI, 689; Gerard, *ibid.*, VII, N. S., 237–238; Hodge, *Handbook*, I, 547.

25. See Friederici, *Hilfswörterbuch*, pp. 59–60 (1926).

26. Consult Swanton, *B.A.E.*, Bul. 43, pp. 279–281 (1911); Hodge, *Handbook*, Part II, 24 (1910).

27. Margry, *Mémoires*, IV, 113, *et passim*.

28. *Jour. Hist.*, pp. 9, 10, 13 (1821).

29. Chamberlain, *Amer. Anthrop.*, N. S., III, 677; Gerard, *ibid.*, N. S., IX, 100.

30. See Margry, *Mémoires*, III, 287.

31. *Histoire*, III, 134 (1744).

32. *Voyages*, II, 337 (1807). Cf. Du Pratz, *Histoire*, II, 94 (1758).

33. Cf. Hardin, "The First Great River Captain," the *La. Hist. Quar.*, January, 1927, map facing page 48.

34. *Handbook*, II, 205 (1910).

35. *B. A. E.*, Bul. 43, pp. 302 ff. (1911).

36. See the New Orleans *Times-Picayune* for Sunday, Dec. 27, 1925.

37. *Amer. State Papers*, Pub. Lands, II, 791. G. & S.

38. *Amer. Anthrop.*, N. S., X, 101 ff.

39. Cf. *Amer. Anthrop.*, N. S., I, 162 ff.; *ibid.*, N. S, I, 790–791.

40. Gerard, *Amer. Anthrop.*, N. S., IX, 102.

41. *Travels and Works of Captain John Smith*, I, 355 (1910).

42. *Histoire*, II, 93 (1758).

43. *Louisiana Studies*, p. 184 (1894).

44. *Louisiana*, I, 145 (1914).

45. See J. Fair Hardin, in the *La. Hist. Quar.*, January, 1927, pp. 49 ff.

46. *Annals of Congress*, 9th Cong., 2d sess., col. 1076. Washington, 1852.

47. *History of Louisiana*, p. 14 (1882).

48. *Jour. Hist.*, p. 21 (1831). On Le Sueur, cf. Margry, *Mém.*, VI, 55 ff. *La Harpe, Op. Cit., p. 27, has *Tigouiclou*.

49. Cf. Peter A. Brannon, "Some Peculiarities in Alabama Names," *Alabama Dept. of Archives and History*, Bul. for April, 1926, pp. 54–55.

3

[76] Indian Words (from *Louisiana French* by William A. Read, 1931)

Historical—At the close of the seventeenth century, the early French colonists found the Lower Mississippi Valley and the adjacent territory in the possession of numerous Indian tribes, who are classified as members of four great linguistic families, the Caddoan, the Muskhogean, the Siouan, and the Tunican. Beginning slightly west of Pearl River and extending eastward through what is now Middle and Southern Mississippi, and reaching a line at some distance beyond the Tombigbee River, was the territory of the powerful Choctaw nation. The French soon entered into fairly intimate relations with the Choctaws, who at that time numbered about 15,000 souls, and who during the latter part of the eighteenth century drifted in bands, more or less numerous, across into Louisiana. From the Choctaw language the French borrowed more words directly than from any other Indian source, a fact that may be ascribed partly to the numerical superiority of the Choctaws over other Southern tribes, and partly to the close kinship of Choctaw with the Mobilian dialect. The *Mobilienne,* thus named by the French after Mobile, the great trading post of the Colonial Period, served as a medium of communication for all the tribes of the Lower Mississippi Valley,[1] and extended its influence as far north even as the mouth of the Ohio. It was as important to the Indians and white traders of the Colonial Period as French is today to the diplomatic [77] circles of Europe. To British traders it became known as the Chickasaw trade jargon, because of the close resemblance between the Chickasaw and the Choctaw or Mobilian vocabulary. Now the Mobilian is based chiefly on Choctaw, and contains indeed so much of the Choctaw vocabulary that this circumstance proved

5. Map of linguistic stocks of American Indians

to be decisive in rendering the influence of Choctaw greater on the French language than that of any other Indian dialect. A few Choctaws still live in St. Tammany Parish, and four Choctaw families occupy the Whatley farms near Jena, in La Salle Parish. More than a thousand Choctaws are in Mississippi. In 1925 the Choctaw Nation in Oklahoma was estimated at 26,828. It should be borne in mind, furthermore, that the Mobilian was enriched by loans from the dialects of Algonquian tribes who inhabited the region lying to the north of the Southern Indian territory.

Besides the Choctaw or Mobilian element there is another class of significant Indian loans in Louisiana-French. These are the words, either Algonquian or Iroquoian in origin, which were brought to Louisiana by Acadians and Canadians, by missionaries, *voyageurs,* and *coureurs de bois.* The territory of the Algonquians formerly comprised almost all of Canada east of the one hundred and fifteenth meridian and south of Hudson's Bay, as well as that part of the United States lying east of the Mississippi and north of Tennessee and Virginia. In 1907 there were about 90,000 Algonquians, a majority of whom are now distributed at various points throughout Canada. At the coming of the white men the Algonquian territory surrounded that of the Iroquois, another extensive linguistic family, whose northern tribes once occupied the region extending from the shores of the St. Lawrence, Lakes Huron, Ontario, and Erie as far south as the present state of Maryland. The present population of the Iroquois is estimated at 16,000 or 17,000 souls, of whom two thirds are settled at various places in the provinces of Quebec and Ontario.

It is important to remember, in the next place, that the French first used the name *Acadie* to distinguish the east[78]ern part of New France from the western, which began with the St. Lawrence Valley and was called *Canada.* The ancient province of Acadia comprises approximately parts of Maine and the province of Quebec, as well as the provinces of New Brunswick, Nova Scotia, and Prince Edward Island. When a settlement was effected in 1605 at Port Royal, now Annapolis, in Nova Scotia, by the Sieur de Monts, Champlain, and other noted Frenchmen, all this region formed the hunting grounds of Algonquian tribes known as the Abnakis, the Micmacs, and the Malecites. Survivors of these tribes still inhabit parts of the Ancient Acadia. Indian words, therefore, which survive in the Acadian dialect are likely to be of Algonquian origin; whereas those met with in the dialect of western Canada may be either Algonquian or Iroquoian.

Unfortunately, it is difficult to determine, from the writings of the French explorers, exactly when an Indian word reached Louisiana. Now and then, it is true, an Indian loan is mentioned in such a way as to prove beyond question that it was brought to the Lower Mississippi region long before any Acadian exile ever set foot on the soil of his new home. Thus Pénicaut speaks of *mitasses* as one of the presents given by Iberville in 1699 to the chiefs of five Southern tribes, and he adds that the Canadians in their party showed the Indians how to put on these *mitasses,* or "leggings."[2] In this connection one will recall that the edict of exile was not issued against the Acadians until 1755; and that perhaps ten years passed before any Acadians settled in Louisiana. Occasionally one comes across an

Indian word in a work that was published after the arrival of some of the Acadians in Louisiana; but the reference to such a word simply fixes the *terminus ad quem*, and leaves us in the dark as to the *terminus a quo*. The writers on Indo-Canadian words are here of little help, being often content to say nothing about the particular locality in which Indian words are found. The exact provenience of these Indo-Canadian words is a problem that needs further investigation.

[79] The French language of Louisiana has drawn, as has been seen, on the vocabulary of the Choctaw or Mobilian, the Algonquian, and the Iroquoian dialects. It has also borrowed a few words from various other sources, notably Carib, Malay, Mexican, and South American. Some of these words came into Louisiana-French through the medium of Spanish, *supra*. One or two Malay words are here grouped with the Indian for lack of a more suitable place.

Let us look now at the Indian words used in Louisiana-French. That the total number of Indian loans is small will not surprise any one who reflects on the vast difference between the structure of the French language and that of an Indian dialect. Moreover, the French colonists, considering themselves in every respect superior to the Indians, naturally borrowed as a rule only those words that designate place names and objects peculiar to the New World.

ACADIEN, -ienne, *sb., adj. Acadien,* "Acadian," is formed from *Acadie,* the ancient French name of Nova Scotia. The exact origin of *Acadie,* which was early Latinized to *Acadia,* has never been solved.[3]

Acadien is often shortened to *Cadien* and the latter is frequently pronounced *Cajē. Cajē* may be derisive in tone, as not seldom in *Il est un Cajē,* "he is a Cajun," or in *il parle Cajē,* "he speaks Cajun."

AÇMINE, *f.* The fruit of the papaw tree; a syncopated form of *acimine.*[4]

An earlier form than Charlevoix's is *racemina* (1772), which is derived from Illinois (Algonquian) *rassimina,* a compound of *rassi,* "divided lengthwise in equal parts," and *mina,* "seeds."[5]

AÇMINIER, *m.* The Pawpaw Tree (*Asimina triloba* Dunal). The proper form is *acminier,* as used by Charlevoix, *Histoire,* III, 395. Du Pratz writes it *Asseminier.*[6]

Açminier and *açmine* (the fruit) are sometimes heard at Marksville, according to Miss Velma Barbin; [80] but the usual terms are *jasmine* and *jasminier. Jasmine* and *jasminier* are also used at Lafayette, I am informed by Miss Ann Spotswood Buchanan. Cf. *jasminier, infra.*

ACOLAN, *m.* I have not succeeded in finding any Creole or Acadian who is familiar with *acolan*, "petticoat"; but the word occurs, as Friederici has pointed out,[7] in Baudry des Lozières' *Voyage à la Louisiane* (1802), p. 211, where one reads of Indian women who wear "un petit jupon de drap qui pend jusqu'aux genoux, et qu'on appelle, à la Louisiane, *acolan.*"

Acolan is a corruption of Choctaw *álhkuna*, "gown," "dress for a lady." Dumont observes that the married women alone were permitted to wear the little skirt which they called *un Alconand.*[8] Perhaps some Creole of the older generation may remember this variant, which is much closer to the Indian source than *acolan.* The Indian word may have survived in the French language of Louisiana as late as 1862; for in that year the anonymous author of an *Essai sur Quelques Usages et sur l'Idiome des Indiens de la Basse Louisiane* gives, on page 56, the phrase *Vêtements de femme* as the equivalent of Indian *Alcouna.*

BABICHE, *f.* A rawhide, especially one that is hard and stiff; or also a strip cut from a rawhide, a thong. The word is used figuratively, too, as in the sentence *Il (elle) est raide comme une babiche*, "He (she) is as tough as a rawhide." My attention was first called to this word by Mr. Phillip Brignac, of French Settlement, in Livingston Parish; subsequently his definition of *babiche* was corroborated by my colleague, Professor Frank Guilbeau, whose dialect was formed chiefly in the parish of St. Martin.

Canadian-French *babiche,* the immediate source of the La.-Fr. word, is defined as the term for a "narrow strip of leather, eelskin, etc.";[9] and it is said to be an aphetic derivative of Algonquian *sisibab*, "cord," or rather *sisibabish*, "a little cord."[10] Another highly probable source is Cree *Assababish,* the diminutive of *Assabab*, "thread."[11] Again, the Nipissing dialect has *nababish* [81] in the sense of a little strip of rawhide with which the Indians sew their moccasins; and Micmac has *abebe*, "rope." Lescarbot spells the word *ababich,* which he renders by "corde ou fil."[12] The French-Canadians use strips of eel skin in making snowshoes.

The La.-Fr. homonym *babiche,* as used contemptuously in such an expression as *une grosse babiche,* "a big mouth," or *Ferme ta babiche,* "shut your mouth," is connected with the echoic stem *bab-, found in *babiller,* "to babble," *baboue*, "grimace," and similar French words. The French dialects of Vendée and the Centre have *babiche,* "lip"; the dialect of Mons has *babiches,* "big lips."[13] As to French *babiche,* "lap-dog," I note that it seems to be generally replaced in Louisiana by *caniche, f.,* literally "poodle-dog." This third *babiche* is a hybrid derivative of the stem **bab-,* "to babble," and French *barbichet,* "little poodle-dog."[14]

BACHOUCTA, *m.* Dye made from the foliage of the Smooth, Upland, or Scarlet Sumac (*Rhus glabra* L.). Some Acadians in the Southwest still color their yarn with this dye. The source of *Bachoucta* is Choctaw *bashuk-sha,* "sumac." The vowels and consonants in *Bachoucta* have the values assigned to them in French.

BATISCAN. The Canadians use *batiscan* as a mild oath to express surprise, regret, scorn, or discontent. Its Standard-French equivalent is *sapristi.*

Batiscan* is apparently the same word as *Batiscan,* the name of a tributary of the St. Lawrence. Champlain mentions the Batiscan River as early as 1603.

In a dialect of the Montagnais, an Algonquian tribe living in Canada, *patiscan* signifies "vapor," "light mist." The same word is also said to be used in the sense of "dried meat," from which the Indians prepared their pemmican.[15]

Baraga derives *batiscan*—less plausibly, I think—from Cree *Tabateskan,* "split horn," "hanging horn," or from Cree *nabateskan,* "one horn."[16]

Canadian *batiscan* seems to be a rare word in Louisiana-French. My friend, Dr. E. O. Trahan, however, is familiar with *batiscan,* which he has heard in Southwest Louisiana.

[82] BAYOU, *m.* The term *bayou* is generally applied to a sluggish stream that is smaller than a river and larger than a *coulée.* Historic Bayou Teche, however, is about 175 miles long, and it widens into a river near its junction with the Atchafalaya. Though a bayou may serve to connect one stream, or body of water, with another, a glance at a map of Louisiana will show that such a condition is far from being invariable. Moreover, a bayou sometimes changes the direction of its current according to the amount of rainfall in its vicinity. Standing on the bridge at Hope Villa, in Ascension Parish, one may see Bayou Manchac flowing eastward towards the Amite River; but when the Amite is swollen by heavy rains, the bayou sets westward towards its former source, the Mississippi. A bayou of course remains stationary when it attains, as Bayou Manchac often does, the same height as that of the stream into which it ordinarily empties.

Bayou,* in spite of the formal resemblance to French *boyau,* "bowel," is not related to this French word. The sole origin of bayou is unmistakably Choctaw *bayuk,* "creek," "river."[17]

BOUCANE, *f.;* Boucaner, *vb. tr., intr.;* Boucanière, *f. Boucane* is the usual La.-Fr. equivalent of French *fumée,* "smoke." Thus one says, *La cuisine est remplie de boucane,* "The kitchen is filled with smoke"; *Il voit la boucane d'un bateau à vapeur,* "He sees the smoke of a steamboat."

The verb *boucaner* is a transitive, as in *boucaner de la viande, du poisson, du tabac,* "to smoke-dry meat, fish, tobacco"; an intransitive, as in *La cheminée boucane,* "The chimney smokes," *Le poêle boucane,* "The stove smokes," etc.

Boucanière is Louisiana-French for "smoke-house." With the termination of *boucanière* one may compare that of *cyprière,* "cypress forest," *pacanière,* "pecan grove," and similar forms. But if French *boucanier,* "buccaneer," is used in Louisiana, it has escaped my attention: its place is taken by French *pirate* or *flibustier.*

Boucan, m., Boucanerie, f., and *Boucanière* are Canadian-French designations of a "smoke-house." *Boucane* and *boucaner* are likewise common in Canadian-French, and the latter is found in the writings of the French explorers of the seventeenth century. Thus Nicolas de la Salle, in his description of the Cavelier de la [83] Salle's discovery, in 1682, of the Mississippi, makes the following reference to a band of savages that La Salle's party encountered not very far south of the Oumas: "They fled to their village, leaving their fishing and a basket that contained a fish, a man's foot, and a child's hand, all smoked (*boucané*).[18] Pénicaut, too, comments briefly on the manner in which the savages prepared their meat: "Their meat is ordinarily smoked or *boucanée,* as one says in that country."[19]

Boucan is not, as is generally thought, a Carib word. The French adventurers of the sixteenth century borrowed it from South-American Tupi, a dialect in which *bucán* signifies a wooden lattice frame for the smoking of meat.[20]

The verb *fumer,* "to smoke," is applied in Louisiana, as in France, to the act of smoking tobacco, a pipe, a cigar, etc.: *Fumer du tabac, une pipe, un cigare,* etc. Similarly, *Une personne qui ne fume pas,* "A person who doesn't smoke," is correct both in Louisiana and in France.

CANADIEN, -enne, *adj. Canadien* is naturally a familiar term in Louisiana-French, the Canada goose, for example, being commonly known as *l'oie canadienne* (*Branta canadensis canadensis* L.). Other names for this wild fowl are *l'outarde,* properly "the bustard," and *la barnache,* "the barnacle goose."

French *Canada, m.,* the geographical name from which the adjective is formed, is derived from Iroquois *kanata,* "city," "village," "camp."

CANARI, *m. Canari,* "clay pot," seems to have disappeared from the language of the Creoles, though it survives in the following negro-French refrain:

> Ya pas bouillon pou vos, macommère;
> Canari cassé dans difé (bis);
> Bouillon renversé dans difé.
> Ya pas bouillon pou vous, macommère;
> Canari cassé dans difé.

> ("There's no soup for you, my gossiping friend;
> The pot's broken in the fire;
> The soup is spilled in the fire," etc.)[21]

[84] Marbot, the author of *Les Bambous* (new edition, 1869), notes on page 36, 137, that *canari* occurs in the native dialect of Martinique, and John Bigelow finds the word in Haitian proverbs, such as

> Moune connait ça qua bouilli nen canari li
> ("Every one knows what is boiling in his own pot")
> and
> Canari vlé rîé chôdier
> ("The earthen pot wishes to laugh at the iron pot.")[22]

Canari is a corruption of *canálli,* the Carib name of large earthen pots in which the Carib Indians made their wines.[23]

The Indian women of Louisiana also made large clay pots, in which enough sagamité was cooked at one time for two or three families.[24]

CANTAQUE, *m.* Smilax—*Smilax laurifolia* L., or perhaps *Smilax Bonanox* L.; its large tuber served as food for the Indians and early settlers.[25] These tubers were reduced to powder and mixed with cornmeal or flour. *Cantaque* is still known to some of the older French natives of Southwest Louisiana. This word is derived from Choctaw *kantak,* "smilax." Compare Choctaw *kantak páska,* "brier-root (smilax) bread."

CASSINIER, *m. Cassinier* is the La.-Fr. name of the Yaupon (*Ilex Cassine Walt.* 1788, or *Ilex vormitoria* Ait.), a shrub or small tree, which thrives in

Louisiana and from whose leaves the Indians of the Gulf Coast formerly prepared a famous black drink for use on all festive and ceremonial occasions. This black drink, named thus by British traders, was held in such esteem by the Southern tribes that they never went to war without drinking it in huge quantities. "All the Allibamons," says Bossu,

> drink the Cassine; this is the leaf of a little tree which is very shady; the leaf is about the size of a farthing, but dentated on its margins. They toast these leaves as we do coffee, and drink the infusion of them with great ceremony. When this diuretic potion is prepared, the young people go to present it in [85] Calebashes formed into cups, to the chiefs and warriors, that is the honorables, according to their rank and degree. The same order is observed when they present the Calumet to smoke out of: whilst you drink they howl as loud as they can, and diminish the sound gradually; when you have ceased drinking, they take their breath, and when you drink again, they set up their howls again. These sorts of orgies sometimes last from six in the morning to two o'clock in the afternoon. . . .
>
> The women never drink of this beverage, which is only made for the warriors.[26]

Cassinier is derived from *cassine, f.,* the name given to the black drink by a Timucuan tribe of Florida. In the sixteenth century the Timucua formed the largest and most powerful Indian confederacy in Florida. Laudonnière gives the Indian name of the drink as *Casine;*[27] Le Challeux spells it *cassinet,* according to Paul L. J. Gaffarel's *Histoire de la Floride Française* (1875), p. 462; Francisco Pareja, citing Laudonnière and De Gourges, calls the drink *Cassine* and *Casine.*[28] Cristobal Colon may have been acquainted with the yaupon, for which the Spanish is *casina.*[29]

I have not met any Creoles or Acadians who are familiar with *cassine,* or who brew the drink that the word denotes; yet as late as 1879 Chahta-Ima (Father Rouquette), in *La Nouvelle Atala,* p. 29, mentions *la cassine* as one of the trees of Louisiana. *Cassinier,* on the other hand, is still well known to the citizens of French Settlement, in Livingston Parish, and it has been heard occasionally by Mr. A. Lovell, whose address is Theriot, in Terrebonne Parish.

Charlevois calls the yaupon *Cassine, f.,* or *Apalachine, f.,*[30] deriving the latter term from *Apalachée,* the name of a native tribe of Florida which formerly occupied the region extending from the neighborhood of Pensacola eastward to Ocilla River. The chief towns of this tribe were near the sites of the present Tallahassee and St. Marks. *Apalachée* is from the Hitchiti dialect and signifies "those (people) on the other side, shore, or river."[31]

[86] Personal names were freely bestowed on Indians who took prominent parts in black-drink festivals. Thus *Osceola*, the name of a famous Seminole chief, is literally Creek *Assi-yahola*, "Black-Drink Singer"; and a Chitimacha Indian is said to have been called *Wait'i-Kestmic*, "Pounding-up *Cassine*."[32] What is here even more pertinent is the fact that *Lacasine* was an Attakapas chief whose memory is perpetuated by the name of a large bayou in Southwest Louisiana, now spelled *Lacassine*, but formerly *Lacasine, Lacacene*, and *Cassine*.[33] The village of Lacassine, in Jefferson Davis Parish, was apparently named after the bayou. How did the Indian acquire his name? Was it conferred on him by French settlers because he was a noted drinker of cassine, or because his village was situated among yaupon trees? Or, on the other hand, is his name merely a compound of the French article *la* and the French geographical term *cassine*, literally "cottage," "country house," a derivative of Low Latin *cassina?* Not a few Indians have received French names, such as *Antoine, Bernard, Louis* and *Celestin(e)*.[34] The latter view I believe to be correct.

On the yaupon and the drink called *cassine*, one may consult the following additional references: Du Pratz, *Histoire*, II, 45–46; William Bartram, *Travels* (1791), pp. 449–450; Thwaites, *Early Western Travels*, XVII, 50–51; Andrew Ellicott, *Journal* (1814), pp. 286–287; F. W. Hodge, *Handbook*, I, 150; *ibid.*, II, 1000 f.; John R. Swanton, *Bur. of Amer. Ethnology*, Bul. 73 (1922), 313, 374–375, 394–95; Georg Friederici, *Hilfswörterbuch für den Amerikanisten* (1926), p. 13; Caroline Dormon, *Forest Trees of Louisiana, and How to Know Them*, Bul. No. 15 (Department of Conservation), 69.

CHACTA, *m.* and *f. Chacta* is used not only in the sense of "Choctaw," but also in that of "small," "inferior," as in *une cabane Chacta, un cheval Chacta.* The plural is *Chactas*.

I know of no grounds for the view that Choctaw *Chahta*, the source of French *Chacta*, is corrupted from [87] Spanish *chato*, "flat," though it is true that the Choctaws were accustomed to flatten the heads of their infants.

It was customary for other Southern tribes to flatten the heads of infants. "As they were looking for him [Prudhomme] they fell in with two Chikasas savages, whose village was three days' inland," says Tonti. "They have 2,000 warriors, the greatest number of whom have *flat heads*, which is considered a beauty among them, the women taking pains to flatten the heads of their children, by means of a cushion which they put on the fore-head and bind with a band, which they also fasten to the cradle, and thus make their heads take this form. When they grow up their faces are as big as a soup plate. All the nations on the sea-coast have the same custom."[35]

CHAGANON, Chaouanon, *m.* A bob-tailed chicken, literally a "Shaw-nee chicken." The Algonquian tribe known as the Shawnee formerly in-habited South Carolina, Tennessee, Pennsylvania, and Ohio. Gatschet gives their name as *sáwanó*, "southerner," with the plural *sawanógi.* Two Menominee forms for "south," "southerner," are *sawano* and *shawano.*[36] Why the term "Shawnee" was conferred on a bob-tailed chicken is not clear.

Tonti uses the form *Chaganon*—once *Chagenon*—in his *Mémoire;* but he has *Chaouanou* alone for "Shawnee" in his *Nouvelle Relation.*[37]

It may not be without significance in the evolution of La.-Fr. *Chaganon* that *Chaguanos* (1841) and *Saguanós* (1831) have been recorded as Spanish for "Shawnees."[38]

CHAOUI, *m.* The earliest reference that I have found to *chaoui,* the La.-Fr. name of the raccoon (*Procyon lotor lotor* L.), is in Duvallon's *Vue de la Colonie Espagnole* (1803), 101, where *le chaoui* as well as *le pichou* is classed as a species of fox.

When an Acadian wishes to distinguish the dark raccoon of the cy-press swamps from the slightly redder or yellower raccoon of the marshes, he called the former [88] *un chaoui cyprière,* "a cypress-swamp raccoon." The number of raccoons taken in Louisiana during the season of 1926–27 reached the remarkable total of 127,862.[39]

Chaoui is derived from Choctaw or Mobilian *shaui,* "raccoon." The first syllable of *chaoui* sounds like French *chat,* "cat," except that the Acadian "a" is a little more retracted than the French front "a"; the second syllable is ex-actly like French *oui,* "yes"; and the stress lies on the second syllable.

The term *chat sauvage,* by which the early French explorers designated the raccoon, is obsolete in Louisiana; compare, however, *chat, supra.*

CHOC, *m.* Blackbird. *Choc* is pronounced either like English *chock,* or like American *chock* with an unrounded "o." *Choc* is a general term for various species of blackbird. *Choc de bois* designates clearly the Florida grackle; *choc de prairie,* the boat-tailed grackle; and *choc aile rouge,* the red-winged blackbird. *Choc* is found, too, in *pape chock,* one of the names of the orchard oriole. *Pape* is merely the French word for "pope."[40]

I am confident that *choc* arose in imitation of the birds' notes. Nevertheless, I mention the word here because of the bare possibility that it was corrupted from Atakapa *ts'ok,* "blackbird." The apostrophe in *ts'ok* represents the glottal stop.

Parisian *choc,* likewise an echoic word, but related to *chic,* signifies "high life" as well as "a young gentleman of fashion." Compare the La.-Fr. derisive *un beau choc,* "a fine fellow."[41] *Choc* is also extremely common in the phrase *bien choc,* "quite tipsy."

CHOUPIQUE, *m.* The Bowfin (*Amia calva* L.). *Choupique* is almost the only name given in Louisiana to this fish even by those who cannot speak French. Another term sometimes heard is *poisson de marais, m.,* "swamp fish."

The choupique is commonly thought to be of little value as food, but its flesh, if properly salted and smoked, is said to have a delicious flavor.

Choupique is a derivative of *shupik,* "mudfish," the name bestowed on the bowfin by the Choctaws.[42]

[89] CHOUQUECHI, *m. Chouquechi* is used at Marksville, Avoyelles Parish, as the name of the cushaw, a variety of Crookneck Squash (*Cucurbita moschata* Duchesne), according to Mr. G. L. Porterie, of Marksville. The same term is sometimes heard in the Leonville neighborhood, parish of St. Landry.

Chouquechi is pronounced in two syllables and with the vowels and consonants as in French. *Chouquechi* is clearly an adoption of Choctaw *shukshi,* "watermelon," though the Indian word has changed its meaning in the transition to French. The Indian tribes of Lower Louisiana cultivated the pumpkin, the watermelon, the gourd, and the cushaw.

Another term for the "cushaw" is *giraumon patate, m.,* literally "potato pumpkin," which is heard, for example, at Breaux Bridge, False River, French Settlement, Houma, Labadieville, and St. Martinville. Other less popular terms for the "cushaw" are *coucroche, m.,* "crooked neck," which is very common in the eastern part of St. Landry; *giraumon confiture, m.,* "preserve-pumpkin," which is occasionally used at Opelousas, Houma, Labadieville, and doubtless other towns; and *cushaw,* which has been adopted from English and generally pronounced like French *coucha, m.,* by the farmers of Evangeline Parish. The information about *cushaw* I owe to the kindness of Mr. L. L. Perrault, of Opelousas. I have myself heard *cushaw* pronounced as in English by natives of Pointe Coupée. *Cushaw*, which is also written *cushaw* and *kershaw*, came into English from Virginia Algonquian *escushaw*; compare Cree *askisiw*, "it is raw or green." In some parts of the Southwest *cacha*, *m.*, with a French pronunciation, is the usual term.

Yet another term that is often used in Pointe Coupée for the cushaw is *giraumon* (*à*) *cou*, *m.*, "neck pumpkin." It reminds one of Du Pratz's comparison of the cushaw to a hunting horn. Du Pratz, however, does not distinguish the cushaw from the pumpkin, including both under the term *giromons*, "pumpkins." After observing that one kind of pumpkin is round, he says that another kind is shaped like a hunting horn, is sweeter and firmer, contains fewer seeds, and keeps longer than the other. His term *corps de chasse*, by the way, is erroneous for *cor de chasse*, "hunting horn." He also men[90]tions several ways in which *giromons*, "cushaws," were cooked, dwelling upon the fact that they were fashioned like pears or other fruit and preserved with sugar.[43]

Standard French *giraumon*(*t*), *m.*, the usual Louisiana-French term for "pumpkin," the fruit of the vine *Cucurbita pepo* (L.), is occasionally followed by the word *boeuf* (Livingston Parish), which then has the force of an adjective, "big," "enormous," "extraordinary." As *boeuf* is here invariable, the plural is *les giraumon*(*t*)*s boeuf.* A similar usage of *boeuf* prevails in Canada and in the colloquial speech of France. The final *f* is pronounced in *boeuf.*[44]

Giraumon(*t*) is of unknown origin.

The Creoles also use St.-Fr. *citrouille* for "pumpkin," and St.-Fr. *potiron* for "cushaw."

GRIVE Chéroki(s), *m.* Towhee, Cherokee Robin, or Swamp Robin (*Pipilo erythrophthalmus erythrophthalmus* L.). As this bird becomes very fat in winter, it is also called *grasset* or *grassel*, "fatty," "plump."[45]

St.-Fr. *grive*, "thrush," is used in Louisiana-French as the name of the American Robin (*Planesticus migratorius migratorius* L.).

The original settlements of the Cherokee Nation, a powerful Iroquoian tribe, were on the head waters of the Savannah and Tennessee rivers.

Chéroki(s) is thought to be a derivative of Choctaw *Chalákki*, "Cherokee," which is in turn a corruption of Choctaw *Chiluk-okla*, "Cave dwellers," the term alluding to the fact that some Cherokees formerly lived in caves. Pénicaut spells the tribal name *Cheraquis* in 1659.[46]

JASMINE, *f.* The fruit of the Pawpaw Tree (*Asimina triloba* Dunal).
Compare N. Bossu's comment, in *Nouveaux Voyages*, Pt. II (1768), 154:
"The Jasmine has the form and color of a lemon; it is odoriferous, and
tastes like fig bananas; its seeds resemble beans. The jasmine is poisonous
to hogs."

Under the name *la jasmine* Bossu clearly refers to the fruit of the papaw.
He is mistaken, however, in thinking that it is poisonous to hogs.

[91] The initial *j* in *jasmine* may be due to popular confusion with
French *jasmin*, "jasmine," or to dissimilation of *z-s* to "*j*"-*s* in the plural
combination *les acimines*; *cf. açmine, supra.*

In a somewhat similar manner folk etymology developed obsolete French
danser les jolivettes from *danser les olivettes* "to dance the olive dance."[47]

The word *Natchitoches*, I recall here, which is familiar as the name of a
town and parish in Louisiana, is Caddo Indian for "pawpaws."

JASMINIER, *m.* The Papaw tree; cf. *jasmine, supra.* Miss Velma Barbin,
of Marksville, first called my attention to the fact that *jasminier* and *jasmine* are still used in Louisiana-French.[48]

LATANIER, *m.* Pénicaut observes in 1699 that the cabins of the Pascagoula Indians "were made of earth, and of a round shape, somewhat like
our wind-mills, the roofs being generally covered with bark; but some were
covered with a species of leaf, which is called, in this country, *latanier* (*palmetto*), a shrub peculiar to the country."[49] The Indian women, according to
Du Pratz, made of the palmetto leaves hats as light as an ounce, hooded
coats for themselves, and other pretty things.[50]

The huts of fishermen, hunters, and loggers are still sometimes covered
with the leaves of the dwarf palmetto (*Sabal adansonii* Guerns.), a low gre-
garious palm, with large fan-shaped leaves, which is extremely abundant in
Southern and Lower Louisiana. It is Robin's *Palmier nain*, "dwarf palm,"
or *Latanier.*[51]

A bayou by the name of *Latanier* is situated not far from the village of
Richland, in Rapides Parish. See survey T 3 N, R 1 E, La.-Mer., 1807.

Seventeenth-century *latanier*, which was Latinized to *Latania* by Com-
merson in 1789, is a French derivative of Carib *aláttani*, the name of a
small fan-leaf palm.[52]

[92] MARINGOUIN, *m. Maringouin*, "mosquito," is a derivative of
South American Tupi and Guarani *marigoui* or *maringouin*. For references

on the history of *maringouin*, see especially Friederici, *Hilfswörterbuch*, p. 61.

The earliest example of *maringouin* recorded by the *Dictionaire Général* is taken from the *Relation des Missions* (1655) of Pierre Pelleprat, a Jesuit missionary to Mexico and the West Indies. But in 1632, nearly a quarter of a century before the appearance of Pelleprat's work, Paul Le Jeune speaks of being nearly devoured by the *maringouins* in New France [Canada];[53] and Pierre Boucher, in 1664, says that he regards the *Maringouins*, along with the hostile Iroquois, as the two chief disadvantages of residence in that country.[54] Even more convincing evidence of the Canadians' familiarity with *maringouin* is furnished by a Canadian folk song, a stanza of which runs as follows:[55]

> Si les maringouins te réveillent
> De leurs chansons,
> Ou te chatouillent l'oreille
>   De leurs aiguillons,
> Apprends, cher voyageur, alors
> Que c'est le Diable
> Qui chante tout autour de ton corps
> Pour avoir ta pauvre ame.

Maringouin was not long in making its way down the valley of the Mississippi. Thus the Cavelier de la Salle suffered, according to his own statement, little annoyance from *maringouins* in the country of the Miami Indians.[56] Pénicaut, however, who in 1699 was sailing along the Gulf Coast, had a different story to tell: "We hurried off an hour before daybreak," he said, "to get rid of the annoyance of swarms of small flies or *cousins*, which the Indians call *Maragouins*, and which puncture even to the drawing of blood."[57] This statement of Pénicaut's seems to warrant the conclusion that Southern tribes borrowed *maringouin* from the Canadian travelers—just as the Choctaws adapted *shapo*, "hat," from French *chapeau* and *wak*, "cow," [93] from Spanish *vaca*—or that *maringouin* had early come up the South American coast and reached Louisiana by way of the Antilles. Doubtless this novel word was brought to the lower Mississippi valley not only from Canada but also from the islands. A Haitian proverb runs *Toute cabinette gagne maringouin a yo*, "Every closet has its mosquito," that is, "There's a skeleton in every closet," which my colleague, Professor James F. Broussard, a master of Parisian French, Louisiana-French, and the negro patois, renders for me into the negro-French of Louisiana by *Tout cabinet gē marin-gouin.*[58]

Though *maringouin* and Standard-French *moustique* are both used in Louisiana, they do not signify the same thing in every part of the State, nor are they everywhere equally common. The distribution and the meaning of the two words are indicated with a reasonable degree of accuracy, in the following tables:

TABLE I
Maringouin, "mosquito."

Place	Parish
Colfax	Grant
Grant	Allen
Lake Charles	Calcasieu

TABLE II
Moustique, "mosquito."

Place	Parish
Baton Rouge	E. Baton Rouge
Clinton	East Feliciana
Destrehan	St. Charles
Gramercy	St. James
Louisa	St. Mary
Mandeville	St. Tammany
Pilot Town	Plaquemines
Pointe à la Hache	Plaquemines

[94] TABLE III
Maringouin and *Moustique*
"Mosquito"

Place	Parish
Bayou Goula (*Maringouin* is rare and low colloquial)	Iberville
Des Allemands	Lafourche
Franklin (*Moustique* is the more common)	St. Mary
Golden Meadow (*Maringouin* is rare)	Lafourche
Gueydan	Vermilion
Houma (*moustique* is rare)	Terrebonne

Lafayette (*maringouin* is low colloquial)   Lafayette
Mansfield   De Soto
Marksville (*maringouin* is less common and often
   low colloquial)   Avoyelles
Napoleonville   Assumption
Natchitoches (*maringouin* is rare)   Natchitoches
Paradis   St. Charles
Plaquemine   Iberville
St. Bernard (*maringouin* is rare)   St. Bernard
Thibodaux   Lafourche
Ville Platte   Evangeline

TABLE IV
Maringouin, "large swamp mosquito";
moustique, "small house mosquito."

Place	Parish
Bunkie	Avoyelles
Dutch Town	Ascension
French Settlement	Livingston
La Place	St. John Baptist
New Iberia	Iberia
New Orleans	Orleans
Opelousas	St. Landry
St. Martinville	St. Martin

TABLE V
Maringouin, "mosquito"; *moustique,* "small black gnat."

Place	Parish
Addis	W. Baton Rouge
Maringouin	Iberville
New Roads	Pointe Coupée

[95] TABLE VI
Maringouin, "wiggletail"; *moustique,* "mosquito."

Place	Parish
St. Francisville	West Feliciana

Mangeur Maringouins, "mosquito eater," is one of the names of the Nighthawk or Bull Bat (*Chordeiles virginianus virginianus* Gmel.) and the Florida Nighthawk (*Chordeiles virginianus chapmani* Coues). The Chuck-Will's-Widow (*Antrosfomus carolinensis* Gmel.) is also called *Mangeur Maringouins.*[59]

Can.-Fr. *Mangeur de Maringouins* signifies "Nighthawk."

Here and there in Louisiana, Standard-French *cousin* is occasionally used as a general term for the "mosquito."

Finally, *Maringouin* designates a town and a bayou in Iberville Parish.

MATACHÉ-ÉE, *adj.* This adjective is used in such expressions as *un chien mataché,* "a spotted dog," *une vache matachée,* "a spotted cow," *les coshons matachés,* "the spotted pigs," etc.

Father Du Poisson, writing to Patouillet in the first quarter of the eighteenth century, says that *un peau mataché* is a skin painted in divers colors by savages, a skin on which are represented calumets, birds, and beasts; and he comments, furthermore, on the appearance of a group of savages "arrayed as for a ceremony, carefully *mataché*—that is, with the whole body painted in different colors."[60] Again, Dumont observes that the Indian women are passionately fond of vermilion, which they use for the purpose of besmearing themselves—*pour se mattacher*—applying it not only to the face, but sometimes also to the top of the shoulders and the breast.[61] *Matachiaz,* a noun related to *mataché,* is the equivalent of "necklaces, scarfs, and bracelets," according to Lescarbot (1612–1614).[62] Champlain declares that among the northern tribes *matachias* is the name given to bits of shell polished and strung together in beads.[63]

[96] In Canadian-French *mataché* also signifies "spotted," and it is from Canada that the word must have been brought to Louisiana. Though the exact source of *mataché* has thus far eluded my search, the word seems to be connected with Algonquian *mat-,* a prolific stem that expresses the general idea of passing from action to inaction, as in *mataton,* "to carry a canoe to the water," *matadjimo,* "to begin to speak," *mataige,* "to scrape skins,"—in Ojibway, *madaige,* and in Cree, *mâtahwew.*

The Canadians may have misunderstood the meaning of Cree *mâtahwew,* "to scrape a skin," and corrupted it to *mataché,* applying the term to the colors with which a skin was painted. Perhaps, however, the original signification of the Algonquian term is no longer clear. Thus William Strachey, as A. F. Chamberlain has pointed out, renders English "Perle" by the Indian *Matacawrak* and "a red dye" by the Indian *Mataquiwun,* in the supplement to a *Historie of Travaile into Virginia Britannia.*[64]

Leon Wiener connects *matachiaz* with French *matasse,* "raw silk"—in other words, "a silk string of beads."[65]

The striking resemblance between *mataché* and Span.-Port. *matizar,* "to color," "to beautify,"—cf. Span. *matizado,* "variegated,"—cannot escape the attention of Romance scholars. This resemblance cannot but be purely accidental.

Mr. Émile Picou, of Houma, in Terrebonne parish, first explained to me the meaning of *mataché.* Since my conversation with him I have heard the word in many other parts of Louisiana—in the parishes of East Baton Rouge, Pointe Coupée, Livingston, Iberia, Assumption, St. James, St. Landry, St. Martin, Lafourche, Jefferson, Orleans, and Plaquemines. *Mataché* is probably used wherever French is spoken in Louisiana. The transition in meaning from the Indian "painted in divers colors" to the Canadian "spotted" is easy and natural. The substantive *matachias* seems not to have been preserved in Louisiana-French—nor the verb *se matacher* either.

MICOINE, *f.* Audubon says that he cannot trace the etymology of *Micoine,* the name by which the Creoles of Lower Louisiana designate the Shoveler Duck (*Spatula clypeata* [97] L.).[66] The word is of Indian origin. Lahontan observes that the *Micoine* is a wooden spoon, made with a curved knife, a *Coutagan,* by the savages of Canada.[67] He also gives *Mickouan* as the Algonquian term for a spoon.[68] Again, Du Pratz notes that the savages eat their *Sagamité,* as one eats soup, with a utensil made of a buffalo horn, which is cut in two and fashioned almost like a spoon.[69] Bossu, too, declares that the Indians make *Micouenes* or spoons, as well as powder horns, out of the buffalo horn.[70]

Canadian-French *micoine* or *micoinée, f.,* "large spoon," is corrupted from Algonquian *emikwan,* the name of a wooden spoon made in various shapes and sizes.[71] The Canadians brought the word to Louisiana and applied it to the shoveler duck, whose bill is wide enough at the end to scoop up the mud in the manner of a spoon. *Micoine*—I have never heard *micoinée*—maintains its French pronunciation, *mi-* riming with French *si* and *-coine* with French *moine.* The stress is on the second syllable. It may not be without interest to recall that the Biloxi-Indian word for "hoe" is *mikōni.*

MITASSES, *f. pl.* Leggings, puttees, as in *une paire de mitasses*, or, in a transferred sense, as in *une poule à mitasses*, "a hen with feathers on its legs." The word is well known among the French of Louisiana.

In 1699 Pénicaut describes the *mitasses* as garments made of half a yard of cloth, cut in two and sewed together like a pair of stockings, through which the Indians pass their legs.[72] Baudry des Lozières observes that the *mitas* which are worn by the Indian men in winter are a kind of gaiter, made of very fine skin and ornamented with little bells, which make a good deal of noise when their wearers are walking.[73] Other references to the word are not rare: compare *mytes*, Pénicaut (Margry, V, 446); *Mitas*, Lahontan, II, 223; *Mitasses*, Du Pratz, II, 196; *une paire de superbes mitasses*, Du Lac, p. 327, and *Mitasses*, p. 349.

[98] *Mitasses* came into Canadian-French from Algonquian (Nipissing or Cree) *mitas*, "leggings," and reached the Gulf Coast more than half a century before the edict of exile was issued, in 1755, against the Acadians. The word is found in several Algonquian dialects, two curious forms being Ojibway *Mittaous*—or *Midass*, according to Baraga—and Menominee *mitiqsan*.[74]

ORANG-OUTANG, *m.* Standard French *Orang-Outang*, the name of an anthropoid ape (*Pithecus satyrus* Geoffroy), inhabiting Borneo and Sumatra, is also used in Louisiana and Canadian-French. The French word is derived from Malay *Orang* (*h*) *utan*, "man (of the) woods," that is to say, "wild man," "jungle-dweller," the native designation of a member of a savage race. Either in jest or through misapprehension the name was given to the ape by Europeans of the seventeenth century.[75]

The first vowel of *orang-outang* is often elided in the Acadian pronunciation. This word doubtless found its way into Louisiana-French from Canada as well as from France.

OUAOUARON, *m.* Lafcadio Hearn cites *ouaouaron*, the La.-Fr. word for the bullfrog (*Rana catesbiana* Shaw), as a delightful and absolutely perfect example of onomatopoeia.[76] This word, however, was not coined in Louisiana; for it is found, Sagard points out, in the Huron dialect, where it takes the form *ouaron*, "gros grenouille."[77] J. A. Cuoq, too, renders Iroquois *iotskwarhohon* by *Il y a bruit de grenouilles; on entend coasser les grenouilles;* and he gives *wararon* as the correct Iroquois name for the bullfrog.[78] There is no doubt, then, that Huron *ouaron* and Iroquois *wararon*, which are alike imitative of the bullfrog's notes, were corrupted by the French of Canada and brought by them to Louisiana in the form *ouaouaron*.

Ouaouaron is pronounced as a French word—usually *wawarō,* but sometimes *warwarō* (Ouararon)—with the stress in each case on the open nasal "o" of the final syllable. The latter pronunciation is said to be the more refined.

[99] French *grenouille,* generally pronounced by the Acadians as if it were written *grounouille* or *gounouille,* signifies in Louisiana any small green frog; it is never used in Acadian, so far as I know, as a designation of the bullfrog.

PACANE, *f.* 1. The pecan nut. Cf. *pacanier, infra.*

The nuts of the pecan tree are more delicate than those of France and less oily, says Du Pratz; their flavor is so fine that the French make pralines of them as good as those of almonds.[79]

The pralines of Louisiana are too well known to require description. Perhaps it should be noted, however, that *praline* is often pronounced as if it were written *plarine;* and that *praline* has helped to render famous the Maréchal du Plessis-Praslin (1598–1675), whose chef was the first to make the candy bearing this nobleman's name. 2. The Least Sandpiper (*Pisobia minutilla* Vieill.). The name *pacane,* "pecan," is conferred on this bird by hunters and guides of South Louisiana because of its small size and color. It is also called *la petite bécassine,* "the little snipe."

Pacane is derived from the generic name for a hard-shell nut in the Algonquian dialects. Compare Cree *pakan,* "nut," and Ojibway *pakan,* "nut," walnut"; *pagan,* "hazel nut." Though *pacane* is also found in Canadian-French, the immediate source of the Louisiana word is doubtless to be sought in the Mobilian, which took the name from some Algonquian dialect.

La pacane amère is a La.-Fr. term for the bitter pecan, the fruit of the Water Hickory (*Hicoria aquatica* Britt.), as well as for the pignut, the fruit of the species *Hicoria glabra* Britt. and *Hicoria cordiformis* Britt.

PACANIER, *m.* "Parmi les fruitiers, qui sont particuliers à ce pays, les plus remarquables sont les Pacaniers, les Aciminiers, & les Piakiminiers," writes Charlevois in October, 1721, describing the country inhabited by the Kaskaskia, once the leading tribe of the Illinois confederacy.[80] Of the trees that he mentions here, two are the pecan and the persimmon; the other variety, which he calls *Aciminiers,* is the North American Pawpaw

(*Asimina triloba* Dunal), though the Acadians of the present day usually speak of this tree as *le jasminier* [100] and of its fruit as *la jasmine, supra*. In M. Lézermes's *Catalogue Alphabétique de Arbres et Arbrisseaux* (Paris, 1788), p. 15, *Assiminier* is given as the name of the pawpaw tree; but Standard French *asiminier* is likewise applied to the West-Indian tree known in English as the Sour-Sop (*Anona muricata* L.). A year and a half before Charlevoix's statement—on May 1, 1720, to be exact—La Harpe, describing his expedition to the Caddo country, gives a lengthy list of the trees he saw there, among which he names the *paganiers* and *plaque-miniers*.[81]

The pecan tree (*Hicoria pecan* Engl. and Graebn.) grows wild in Louisiana, and produces small nuts with sweet kernels; the cultivated pecan, said to be *seeded* or *grafted*, bears much larger nuts of a very fine flavor. The wild pecan is sometimes called *le pacanier sauvage*, or *le pacanier d'aventure*, in contrast with the cultivated variety—*le pacanier greffé* ("grafted"). The bitter pecan or water hickory goes by the name of *le pacanier amer*; so, too, does the pignut, a name generally given to two species of hickory (*Hicoria glabra* Britt. and *Hicoria cordiformis* Britt.).[82] Robin's name for the bitter pecan is *Noyer pacanier amer*.[83]

Ordinarily *le noyer* is the Black Walnut Tree (*Juglans nigra* L.), or the wood of that tree; sometimes, however, it is used as the name of the Hickory (*Hicoria*). When the one is to be distinguished from the other, such terms as *noyer blanc*, "white hickory," and *noyer rouge*, "red hickory," are employed, according to Mr. E. Parent, Jr., of French Settlement. But in Pointe Coupée the hickory is usually called *ikri, m.*, and in Assumption Parish it is *ikré*, both words clearly being deformations of English *hickory*.

Robin describes the black walnut tree as *le Noyer à Fruit noir;* Charlevoix calls it more simply *noyer noir*.[84] Du Pratz groups both the black walnut and certain species of hickory under the name *noyers*.[85]

Pacanier is formed from *pacane, supra*, by the addition of *-ier*. Compare La.-Fr. *La pacanière*, "the pecan grove."

[101] PATASSA, *m. Patassa*, a derivative of Choctaw patàssa, "flat," as used in the phrase *nàni patàssa*, "flat fish," is the generic name of the various species of sunfish that inhabit the fresh waters of Louisiana. Du Pratz, who gives the etymology of the word correctly, observed that the patassa is the *gardon* of the New World.[86] The plural "les patassas" is used by Baudry des Lozières.[87] *Patassa* is pronounced as a French word; but those persons who do not speak French refer to the sunfish by the erroneous term "perch."

At least eight species of sunfish are found in Louisiana; among these the most important are the Bluegill (*Lepomis pallidus* Mitchell), the Scarlet Sunfish (*Lepomis miniatus* Jordan), the Red-breasted Bream (*Lepomis auritus* L.), the Round Sunfish (*Centrarchus macropterus* Lacépède), and the Green Sunfish (*Lepomis cyanellus* Raf.).[88]

PICHOU, *m.* The bob-tailed wild cat, an animal known also as the bobcat, or Bay Lynx (*Lynx rufus Guldenstaed* and *Lynx rufus floridanus* Raf.). In November, 1721, Charlevoix uses the plural *Pijoux* for two species of wild cats: the one with a short tail, which is the common American wild cat; and the other, a larger animal that goes by the name of *cougar* or *puma* (*Felis concolor* L.). The latter is called also *catamount, mountain lion,* and *American lion.* Du Pratz, too, describes the *Pichou,* remarking that it is smaller than the tiger, has a beautiful skin, and is very destructive of poultry; but his illustration of the animal is interesting chiefly because of its total lack of resemblance either to the wild cat or to the cougar.[89]

The wild cat is still met with in the dense forests of Louisiana, whereas the cougar is now almost extinct. The La.-Fr. name for the cougar is *chat-tigre, m.* Duvallon calls the cougar *le tigre Américain.*[90]

Pichou, which is pronounced strictly as a French word, seems to have reached Louisiana in two ways: first, through Mobilian *pishu,* "wild cat," which is taken from Ojibway *bishi, pishiu,* "lynx," or from Menominee *pisheu,* "cougar";[91] and secondly, through Canadian [102] travelers, who borrowed it from Cree *pisiw,* "lynx," or from Nipissing *pishiu,* "lynx," the latter being written *piciw* in Cuoq's *Lexique de la Langue Algonquine,* p. 335, with the translation "loup-cervier," the French term for the Canada lynx (*Lynx canadensis* Geoffroy).

In Canadian-French the word *pichou* designates, as Clapin observes, a person who is ugly or malicious, the phrase *laid comme un pichou* being especially common.[92] In Louisiana an expression often heard is *méchant comme un pichou,* "bad as a wild cat."

From *pichou* has perhaps been formed La.-Fr. *pichouette, infra.*

It is worth adding that Mobilian *pishu* is entirely different from the Choctaw name for the wild cat—that is to say, *shakbatina,* which is formed from Choctaw *shakbona,* "brown," "dusky."

The Choctaw term is appropriate; for the wild cat is reddish-brown in autumn and winter, and ashy-brown in spring and summer, according to

Audubon and Bachman.[93] Compare Latin *rūfus*, which in the scientific term for the wild cat signifies "reddish" of various shades.

PICHOUETTE. *f. Pichouette*, formed perhaps from *pichou*, *supra*, with the aid of the diminutive suffix *-ette*, signifies a "bad little girl," the word being often used in such an expression as *C'est une (petite) pichouette*, "She's a bad little rascal."

Pichouette must not be confused with La.-Fr. *chouette*, "darling," a term of endearment that is related not to French and La.-Fr. *chouette*, "screech owl," but through the Norman dialect to Old French *souef*, "sweet," "gentle" (Gamillscheg). "Ma petite chouette," one says in Louisiana.

Canadian-French *chouette*, too, has the force of *amie*, "sweetheart," and also, like Continental French, of the adjectives "fine," "splendid," "classy." An example of the latter usage is *Cela est chouette*.

The Indian source of *pichouette* is rendered very dubious by the existence, in Southern France, of the personal names *Pichio*, *Pichon*, *Pichot*, and *Pichou*, which L. Larchey renders by (1) *petit enfant, mince, nouveau-né,;* (2) *pie, blanc et noir*.[94] *Pichon* is also a saint's name, equivalent to Latin *Picio*. Moreover [103] *Pichon* signifies "a fish," or "fisherman," in the district lying between Douai and Lille, in Northern France.[95]

Pichon, *Pichot*, and *Pichou* are Canadian family names.[96] Of the three *Pichou* especially is common in Louisiana.

PICOUETTE. *f.* Some Acadians, according to my colleague, Mrs. Judith Major, designate a thin, ill-tempered child by the term *picouette*, saying *c'est une picouette*. The origin of this term is obscure; perhaps it is related, with change of suffix, to Canadian-French *picouille, f.*, "an animal extremely thin, emaciated," which is formed from the Algonquian stem *piko-*, "broken," "shattered," "torn."

PLAQUEMINE, *f.* The fruit of the persimmon tree is called *plaquemine*; the tree itself, *le plaqueminier*, a word which ends in the familiar suffix *-ier*. *Plaquemine* came into Louisiana-French, through the Mobilian dialect, from Illinois *piakimin*, "persimmon."[97] The names for the persimmon tree and its fruit are known to all the French inhabitants of Louisiana.

In Choctaw the persimmon is *ūkof ápi*.

An early reference to the food prepared from persimmons by Indian women is made by Henry de Tonti, who speaks, on November 14, 1684, of "des pastes d'un certain fruit qu'ils appellant *Paquimina,* lequel est fort bon."[98]

PLAQUEMINIER, *m. Plaqueminier* is the name of the persimmon tree (*Diospyros virginiana* L.), which grows almost everywhere in the State. Charlevoix gives the name as *Piakiminier* or *Plakminier de la Floride;*[99] and De Pratz notes the French change of *Piacminier* to *Placminier.*[100] On May 1, 1720, La Harpe uses the modern spelling, in the plural *plaqueminiers.*[101]

For the origin of *plaqueminier,* see *plaquemine, supra.*

SACACOUA, *m.*; Sasacoua, *m.* These words signify "hubbub," "racket," "uproar," "confused cries," "shouts," as defined for me by Messrs. F. V. Brignac, V. Guitrau, [104] and A. Vicknair, all of French Settlement, Livingston Parish. *Sacacoua* has nothing to do with French *saccage,* "confusion," "jumble," but is of Algonquian origin: compare Cree *Sâkowew,* "to utter cries of joy or encouragement," Nipissing *sakwatam,* "to utter cries of joy or encouragement," Nipissing *sakwatam,* "to utter cries," and *sakakwa,* "thick forest," words containing the stem *sak-,* "numerous," "close together," "serrated." *Sacacoua* is pronounced as if written *sakakwa,* the stress normally falling on the last syllable. That Algonquian *sakakwa* was adopted by the French of Canada, to whom it is still familiar and by whom it was brought to the lower Mississippi valley, is evident from the occurrence of the form *sacacayou* in Nicolas de la Salle's narrative of an encounter with a body of Natchez Indians: "Ils firent le sacacayou, la huée," he says, obviously assigning to *sacacayou* the sense of "war-cry."[102] The ending of *sacacoua* is apparently due to confusion with that of *sasacoua, infra.*

SASACOUA, *m.* Another Canadian-French word of the same signification as *sacacoua* is also used in Louisiana—namely, *sasacoua,* which was adopted by the Canadians from Algonquian (Nipissing) *sasakwe,* "to utter piercing cries"; compare Ojibway *sassakwe,* "to shout with joy," Cree *sâkowew, sâsâskwew,* "to utter cries of joy, of encouragement." The form *sasocoüest* is found in Father Membré's narrative of La Salle's voyage down the Mississippi. "Having sailed forty leagues till the third [or 13th] of March [1682]," writes Membré, "we heard drums beating and sasocoüest (war-cries) on our right. Perceiving that it was an Akansa village, the Sieur de la Salle immediately passed over to the other side with all his force, and in less than an hour threw up a re-trenched redoubt on a point, with pali-

sades and felled trees, to prevent a surprise and give the Indians time to re-
cover confidence."[103] *Sasacoué* is a Canadian-French variant.

Sacacoua is used at Bayou Goula, Convent, French Settlement, Jones-
ville, and Kinder; *sasacoua*, at Clinton, Loreauville, Marksville, and New
Iberia; in the parish of Point Coupée and in the city of New Orleans. Obviously, a city as large as New Orleans may also num[105]ber among its
residents some who are familiar with *sacacoua* rather than with *sasacoua*.
But in many communities neither form of the word is known.

Folk etymologists are inclined to resolve *sacacoua*, which is pronounced
sakakwa, into *sac à quoi*, and sometimes they apply the term to a braggart,
taking *C'est un sacacoua* to be the equivalent of "He's a windbag." Ordinarily, however, *sacacoua* as well as *sasacoua* has the same meaning as *tapage*
and *vacarme*, "great noise," words which are naturally as common in Louisiana as they are in France.

SACAMITÉ, *f. Sagamité* is the name of the hominy or porridge that
the Indians made of coarse Indian corn; with the hominy they sometimes
boiled meat, or fish, or beans. The popularity of this dish attracted the attention of many early explorers of the New World. Bossu once dined with
the Peoria Indians on bears' paws, beavers' tails, and a kind of bread which
the Indians called *pliakmine*. (Cf. *Plaquemine, supra.*) "I likewise eat," he
says, giving further details about the dinner, "of the dog's flesh through
complaisance, for I have made it a rule to conform occasionally to the ge-
nius of the people with whom I am obliged to live, and to affect their man-
ners, in order to gain their friendship: they likewise brought in a dish of
boiled gruel, of maize flour, called *sagamité*, sweetened with syrup of the
maple tree; it is an Indian dish which is tolerably good and refreshing. At
the end of the repast they served a des(s)ert of dry fruits which our Frenchmen called *bluets* (huckleberries; blueberries), and which are as good as
Corinth raisins: they are very common in the Illinois country, which is red
all over with them in the season. The village of the Peorias is situated on
the banks of a little river, and fortified after the American manner, that is,
surrounded with great pales and posts."[104]

No Indian tribe, one should observe, ever conferred the name *sagamité*
on its hominy. As early as 1632, however, the word *sagamité* appears in
Canadian-French through a misapprehension of the meaning of Ojibway
kisagamitew or of a similar form in some other Algonquian dialect. Algonquian (Nipissing) *kijagamite*, according to Cuoq, signified "the liquid (or
water) is hot," the component elements being *agami*, "beverage or soup,"

and *Kiji . . . ite,* "to be boiled." Algonquian [106] *Kij* signifies "heat" or "hot." Lacombe, p. 708, has "*Sagamite* (Cris) pour: *Kisagamitew,* 'C'est un liquide chaud.'" The French Canadians, taking *kijagamite* or *kisagamite* to be the Indian for "porridge," corrupted the word into *sagamité. Sagamité* ultimately found its way through Mobilian to Louisiana, where in the form *sac(c)amité,* "hominy," it is still used by the French. The pronunciation, of course, is French. Another term for *sacamité* is *le gros gru.*

The eighteenth century saw the evolution of such English forms as *shaggamitie, sagamitty,* and *sagamite;* the nineteenth century, *sagamity* as well as *sagamité.* The preferable spelling in English is now *sagamité.*[105]

SOCO, *m.* The French of Louisiana are all familiar with *soco,* the name of the Southern Fox-grape or the berry of the muscadine (*Vitis rotundifolia* Michx.). This grape, which is still fairly common in the forests of Louisiana, is large and round, with a tough skin and a somewhat musky flavor. The jelly made from the muscadine is highly prized. The vine is known as *la liane de soco.* The scuppernong, a variety of the muscadine, is called *soko* or *soko blanc,* "white muscadine."

Choctaw *suko,* "muscadine," is the source of the word. The fact that *suko* has become La.-Fr. *soco*—pronounced *sokó*—doubtless reflects the well-known tendency of Choctaw "u" to interchange with "o," as in *fuka, foka,* "residence," *humma, homma,* "red," *shukulbi, shokolbi,* "nook," *sukolichi, sokolichi,* "to tap," and numerous other words.

TAFIA, *m.* A spirituous liquor obtained from molasses, sugar cane, and brown sugar. Du Pratz speaks of the ardor with which the negroes worked when he promised them "un coup de Tafia."[106] Duvallon observes that the favorite drink of the colonists was *tafia* in which there had been preserved the fruit of the wild cherry tree.[107] The popularity of *tafia* is also attested by the author of *Le Champ d'Asile* (1819), p. 73, note 3.

Mr. L. T. Fontenelle, of Pointe à la Hache, and Mr. L. Falgout, of Raceland, inform me that the word *tafia* is fast becoming obsolete. As late as 1880, however, George W. Cable mentions the syrup and *tafia* that were [107] made from sugar cane;[108] and *tafia* undoubtedly survives in the Louisiana proverb, *Le tafia dit toujours la vérité,* "Tafia always tells the truth." Nowadays, however, Du Pratz's *un coup de Tafia* is ordinarily replaced by *un coup de whisky,* a phrase that the Acadians pronounce *ē kud wiski* (or *uski*). Here *ē* represents the sound of "a" in English *bat* nasalized, and the other letters have the same values as in French.

Tafia is of obscure origin. Though given in 1722 as a native name in the West Indies—"Les sauvages et les nègres l'appellent tafia"[109]—it is, nevertheless, recorded in Malay dictionaries and must have been widely known not only in the West but also in the East. It was admitted to the French Academy in 1762, and is found in English as early as 1777.[110]

From *tafia* has been formed La.-Fr. *tafiateur, m.,* "drunkard."

TAÏQUE, *f. Taïque,* "squaw," is an adaptation both in form and in meaning of Choctaw *tek,* "female," a word which regularly designates the female gender. Thus *isi* is the Choctaw for "deer," whereas *isi tek* signifies "doe." *Taïque* forms the second element in *Faquetaïque,* the name of a prairie in St. Landry Parish and a derivative of Choctaw *fakit tek,* "turkey hen." *Taïk* and *taik* are the spellings used by the anonymous author of an *Essai sur Quelques Usages et sur l'Idiome des Indiens de la Basse Louisiane*—see page 26 *et passim*—which was written at Opelousas in 1862. On page 41 of this essay *taïk* is several times rendered by *femme.* The Howard Memorial Library, in New Orleans, has a copy of this interesting study.

Taïque, which is pronounced strictly in French fashion with the stress on the second syllable, is often employed in a derogatory sense, such an expression as *Elle est mechante comme une taïque,* "She's as bad as a squaw," being not uncommon in Livingston Parish as well as in Lower Louisiana. I have also heard it in the city of New Orleans.

Some Acadians, unfamiliar with the original meaning of *taïque,* use *méchante comme une taïque* with the force merely of *très méchante;* others, equally ignorant ([108]) [109] of the source of *taïque,* assign to it the sense of "a person with long, disheveled hair," saying, for example, *Elle est (comme) une taïque.*

TOMAHAWK, *m.* In Louisiana-French *tomahawk* is rare, being heard, so far as I know, at French Settlement alone, where it signifies "an old hatchet." In Canadian-French it signifies "war-club," and in Chateaubriand's *Atala* (1801) it appears in the sense of "war-ax."

Tomahawk, a word applied to the Indian war-ax, and erroneously also to the war-club, came into English from Virginia Renape *tomahak,* Captain John Smith defining *tomahacks* in 1612 as "axes." Renape *tamahak* is shortened from *tamahakan,* "cutting utensil," which is cognate in turn with Micmac *tumigan,* "ax," Abnaki *tamahigan,* Mohegan *tummahegan,* and similar forms in some other Algonquian dialects.[111] As late as 1874 Lacombe derives Canadian-French *tomahawk* from Cree *otomahuk,* "knock

6. Tomahawk and war-club. From Lahontan's *Mémoires*, II, 193.

him down," or *otamahwaw*, "he is knocked down"; but Standard French borrowed the word from English, and such, too, is, in all probability, the medium through which *tomahawk* reached the French dialect of Canada as well as that of Louisiana. The English form, at any rate, must have helped the Indian word to fix itself in the latter two dialects.

The early French explorers applied the term *casse-tête*, *m.*, first, to the Indian war-club, and afterwards to the little ax that the Indians obtained from white traders. La Salle, awaiting in 1679 the approach of a band of twenty savages, remarks that they were armed with muskets, axes, bows, arrows, and a kind of club called *casse-tête*.[112] Charlevoix, too, defines *casse-tête* as a little club of very hard wood, terminating in a round head with a sharp edge; but he observes further that the same name was subsequently given to little axes which the savages had substituted for the

wooden clubs, and which consequently rendered combats more sangui-
nary.[113] Again, in Lahontan's illustration, reproduced on p. 108 [fig. 6], the
war-club is described as a *Casse-tête*, and the war-ax is distinguished from
it merely by the use of the adjective *petit*.[114]

[110] The information derived from Charlevois and Lahontan is especially interesting because of the light that it throws on the meaning of
casse-tête in Louisiana-French. In this dialect *casse-tête*, literally "break
head," is the only word that corresponds to English *hatchet*. *Hache*, on the
other hand, invariably renders English *ax*.

TOPINAMBOUR, *m.* Jerusalem Artichoke (*Helianthus tuberosus* L.),
and its edible tuber.

French *topinambou* originally designated the name of a native people
of Brazil. From *topinambou* was formed *topinambour*, which received the
meaning of artichoke because the plant is thought to have been first observed in the land of this Brazilian race. The Jerusalem artichoke was cultivated by Indian tribes of the Mississippi Valley before the discovery of
the New World.

Topinambour is found in Canadian as well as in Continental French. In
the seventeenth century it made its way into English, in which it is now
written *topinambou, -bour, -bar*.

In the parish of Iberia *topinambour* is usually pronounced *toupinambour*.

For an excellent comment on the etymology of *topinambour*, see O. Nobi-
ling, "Beziehungen zwischen Europaischen und Amerikanischen Sprachen,"
Revue de Dialectologie Romane, I (1909), 428.

NOTES

1. Fort Louis de la Mobile, established by the French in 1702, on the river Mobile,
was removed in 1710 to the present site of the city of Mobile. The Mobile Indians were
a branch of the Muskhogean family. The tribal name *Mobile* may be connected with
Choctaw *moeli*, "to paddle a canoe." The Choctaws call Mobile *Moilla*. See *A Dictionary of the Choctaw Language*, p. 262.

2. Margry, V, 380.

3. Cf. Eugène Rouillard, *Noms Géographiques da la Province de Québec*, etc. (1906),
pp. 17–18, for a summary of the various interpretations of the name; and my *Louisiana
Place Names of Indian Origin* (1927), pp. 2–3.

4. See Charlevoix, *Histoire*, III, 395.

5. Hodge, *Handbook*, I, 101. See *jasmine, infra*.

6. *Histoire*, II, illustration facing page 20.

7. *Hilfswörterbuch für den Amerikanisten* (1926), p. 1.

8. *Mémoires Historiques de la Louisiane*, I (1753), 138.

9. N. E. Dionne, *Le Parler Populaire des Canadiens Français* (1909), p. 48.

10. M. le Senateur P. Poirier. "Des Vocables Algonquins, Caraïbes, etc., qui sont entrés dans la langue," in *Mémoires de la Société Royale du Canada*, Series III, Tome X (1916), 343.

11. See Baraga, *Dictionary*, I, 298.

12. *Histoire de la Nouvelle France*, III (1612), 666.

13. Wartburg, *Wörterbuch*, p. 192.

14. Gamillscheg, *Wörterbuch*, p. 64.

15. Eugène Rouillard, *Noms Géographiques*, p. 25.

16. *A Dictionary of the Otchipwe Language*, Part I, 298.

17. Compare the writer's *Louisiana Place Names of Indian Origin* (1927), p. XII, and the references there given.

18. Cf. Margry, I, 560.

19. Cf. Margry, V, 390.

20. Georg Friederici, "Vier Lehnwörter aus dem Tupi," *Zeitschrift für Französische Sprache und Literatur*, LIV (1930), 177–180.

21. Lafcadio Hearn, *Gombo Zhèbes* (1885), p. 30, footnote 2.

22. "The Wit and Wisdom of the Haytians," *Harper's Magazine*, Vol. 51 (1875), 585, 586.

23. R. R. R. Breton, *Dictionnaire Caraïbe-Français*, p. 107.

24. Pénicaut (1699), in Margry, V, 389.

25. *Annals of Congress*, 9th Congress, 2nd session (Dec. 1, 1806–March 3, 1807), p. 1107, footnote.

26. Bossu-Forster, I, 249–250.

27. French, *Hist. Coll.*, N. S. (1869), pp. 246, 247, 301.

28. *Arte de la Lengua Timuquana* (1614), XII, XIII.

29. Cf. D. Miguel Colmeiro, *Primeras Noticias acerca de la Vegetación Americana*, (Madrid, 1892), p. 24.

30. *Plantes d'Amérique*, in *Histoire*, II, 29–30; *ibid.*, III, 449–450.

31. Albert S. Gatschet, *A Migration Legend of the Creek Indians*, I, 74.

32. John R. Swanton, in *Bur. of Amer. Ethnology*, Bul. 43 (1911), 353.

33. Cf. *American State Papers*, Public Lands, III, 92, 105, 114, ed. Gales and Seaton; *ibid.*, III, 154, ed. Green; Darby's map of Louisiana, 1816; La Tourette's map of Louisiana, 1846.

34. See *American State Papers*, Public Lands, III, 92, 93, 99, 239, 249, ed. Gales and Seaton.

35. French, *Hist. Coll.* (1846), p. 60.

36. W. J. Hoffman, in *Bur. of Amer. Ethn.*, Rep. XIV, Pt. 1 (1893), 311, 325.

37. See French, *Hist. Coll.* (1846), pp. 69, 71, 72, 74, 75, 77; and *Relations de la Louisiane . . .*, pp. 183, 188.

38. See F. W. Hodge, *Handbook of North American Indians*, II, 537.

39. Stanley C. Arthur, *The Fur Animals of Louisiana*, Bul. No. 18 (Louisiana Department of Conservation, November, 1928), 410.

40. Cf. Stanley C. Arthur, *The Birds of Louisiana* (1918), pp. 60, 61.

41. L. Sainéan, *Langage Parisien*, p. 460.

42. For further information see *The Fresh-Water Fish of Louisiana,* Bulletin 4 (Louisiana Department of Conservation, November, 1917), 15–16; and the writer's *Louisiana Place Names of Indian Origin* (Louisiana State University Bulletin, February, 1927), pp. 24–26.

43. *Histoire,* II, II.

44. Cf. N. E. Dionne, *Le Parler Populaire des Canadiens Français* (1909), p. 80; L. E. Kastner and J. Marks, *A Glossary of Colloquial and Popular French* (1929), p. 47.

45. Cf. Audubon, *Birds,* III, 168.

46. Margry, V, 404.

47. Cf. A. Thomas, *Romania,* XXVIII, 193–194.

48. Note *jasseminier,* in Duvallon, *Vue de la Colonie Espagnole,* p. 112, and in De L'Ain, *le Champ d'Asile* (1819), p. 74.

49. See B. F. French, *Historical Collections,* N. S. (1869), p. 49; Margry, V, 389 ff.

50. *Histoire,* II, 48.

51. *Voyages,* III, 337 ff.; cf. C. S. Rafinesque, *A Flora of Louisiana* (1817), p. 16.

52. Breton, *Dictionnaire Caraïbe-Français,* pp. 243–244.

53. *Jesuit Relations,* V, 36.

54. Benj. Sulte, *Pierre Boucher et Son Livre,* p. 164.

55. See *Roy. Soc. of Canada,* Trans., II, (1896), 97.

56. Margry, I, 465.

57. French, *Historical Collections,* N. S., I (1869), 44; cf. Margry, V, 384. Note, too, Iberville's references to the *maringouins,* Margry, IV, 188.

58. Cf. John Bigelow, in *Harper's Magazine,* LI (1875), 438.

59. Cf. Stanley C. Arthur, *The Birds of Louisiana,* Bul. 5 (Louisiana Department of Conservation, January, 1918), pp. 54, 56.

60. *Jesuit Relations,* LXVII, 256; *ibid.,* LXVII, 251.

61. *Mémoires Historiques,* I (1753), 155.

62. *Jesuit Relations,* II, 134.

63. *Jesuit Relations,* II, 294, note 17.

64. *American Notes and Queries,* II (1888), 3.

65. *Africa and the Discovery of America,* II, 253.

66. *The Birds of America,* VI (1859), 293.

67. *Mémoires de l'Amérique Septentrionale,* II (1728), 215.

68. *Op. cit.,* II, 225.

69. *Histoire,* III, (1758), 9.

70. *Nouveaux Voyages aux Indes Occidentales,* II (1768), 161.

71. Lacombe gives Cree *emikkwán;* Baraga, Ojibway *êmikwân;* Cuoq, Nipissing *emikwan.*

72. See B. F. French, *Hist. Coll.,* N. S. (1869), 40; Margry, V, 380.

73. *Voyage à la Louisiane* (1802), p. 210.

74. See, respectively, Des Lozières, *Voyage,* p. 357; W. J. Hoffman, in *Bureau of American Ethnology,* Rep. 14, Pt. 1 (1893), p. 304.

75. Gamillscheg, *Wb.,* p. 650, cites E. Littmann, *Morgenländische Wörter im Deutschen,* pp. 128 ff.

76. *Gombo Zhèbes* (1885), p. 14, footnote 4.

77. *Le Grand Voyage du Pays des Hurons,* II, 229.

78. *Lexique de la Langue Iroquoise* (1882), p. 140, footnote; *ibid.*, p. 156.

79. *Histoire,* II, 26.

80. *Histoire,* III, 417.

81. See Margry, VI, 265.

82. Cf. *Coteau Pacaniers Amers,* Survey T 14 S-R. 18 E., SE Dist. La., West of Miss. River.

83. *Voyages,* III, 511.

84. *Voyages,* III, 509–510, and *Histoire,* II, App. 48 ff., respectively.

85. *Histoire,* II, pp. 24–26.

86. *Histoire,* II, 156.

87. *Voyage,* p. 175.

88. *Louisiana Today* (1924), p. 76.

89. Cf. Charlevoix, III, 407; Du Pratz, II, 92; Duvallon, p. 101.

90. *op. cit.,* p. 100.

91. Cf. W. J. Hoffman, in *Bureau of American Ethnology,* Rep. 14 (1893), Pt. I, p. 310.

92. *Dict. Canadien-Français,* p. 245.

93. *The Quadrupeds of North America,* I, 2.

94. *Dictionnaire des Noms* (Paris, 1880), p. 375.

95. See Charles Bonnier, *Uber die Französischen Eigennamen in Alter und Neuer Zeit* (1888), p. 14; cf. also Alice Sperber, "zur Bildung Romanischer Kindernamen" *ZRPh., Beih.,* XXVII, 152 ff.

96. N. E. Dionne, *Les Canadiens-Français* (1914), p. 484.

97. See my *Louisiana Place Names of Indian Origin* (1927), pp. 50–51.

98. Margry, I, 601.

99. *Histoire,* II, App., 37; cf. *Piakiminiers, ibid.,* III, 395.

100. *Histoire,* II, 18.

101. Margry, VI, 265.

102. Margry, I, p. 557.

103. Isaac J. Cox, *The Journeys of René Robert Cavelier, Sieur de la Salle,* I, 136.

104. Bossu-Forster, I, 189.

105. Cf. J. A. Cuoq, *Lexique de la Langue Algonquine,* pp. 15–16, 156; F. W. Hodge, *Handbook of American Indians,* II, 407; the *New English Dictionary,* under *sagamité.*

106. *Histoire,* I, 347.

107. *Vue de la Colonie Espagnole* (1803), p. 113.

108. *The Grandissimes,* XVIII, 197.

109. Jean B. Labat, *Voyage aux Îles de l'Amérique,* III, 410.

110. See *A New English Dictionary,* under *tafia.*

111. W. J. Gerard, In *The American Anthropologist,* X, N. S. (1908), 277.

112. Margry, I, 453–454.

113. *Histoire,* III (1744), 222, 238; cf. Du Pratz, II, 200–201 (misprinted 190–191).

114. Lahontan, *Mémoires,* 2 II (1728), facing page 193.

1000 ACTIVITIES

priddy books
big ideas for little people

All about me

My family, friends, pets, hobbies and more.

1 Colour in the family picture when you are ready to start this section.

2 Draw a picture of yourself in the frame.